THERE IS NO ONE PRINCIPLE OF SUCCESS.

Life is not that simple. We all want to succeed in *every* part of our lives. In business, marriage, sex, love, and friendship. To do that, we must understand the things that motivate us toward success—and also understand those things that hinder us. Dr. Joyce Brothers understands people, their motivations, desires, behavior, and psychology. And because she understands people, she understands success—and she knows how to guide *you* to success too.

Do you know what you *really* want?

Which is most important to you: Money? Sex? Excitement? Love? Status? Beauty?

Do you have what it takes to succeed?

What is your success potential? And how can you change it?

Do you know how to get rid of tension in *less* than 60 seconds?

Is your marriage everything it could be?

Do you know the 12-letter dirty word that can get you everything you want?

Also by Dr. Joyce Brothers
Published by Ballantine Books:

WHAT EVERY WOMAN SHOULD KNOW ABOUT LOVE
AND MARRIAGE

WHAT EVERY WOMAN SHOULD KNOW ABOUT MEN

Dr. Joyce Brothers
How to Get Whatever You Want Out of Life

BALLANTINE BOOKS • NEW YORK

Library of Congress Catalog Card Number: 78-14258

ISBN 0-345-34747-1

This edition published by arrangement with Simon & Schuster

Manufactured in the United States of America

First Ballantine Books Edition: February 1980
Eleventh Printing: February 1987

Contents

v

Introduction

This book tries to explain basic psychological principles of human behavior and motivations in such a way that the reader can make use of them in almost any area—marriage, business, sports, politics, sex—in much the same way psychologists use them in practice to help their patients.

Other books in these fields are usually based upon just one principle or approach. But one can never be enough. One manipulative tool to make others do what you want, one psychological effect to make others see you as someone special, one device that you can use to climb the peaks of success is not enough. Life is not that simple. This book contains a whole pharmacopeia of psychological prescriptions to help you get what you want.

I would like readers to consider this as a life resource book, a reference book to turn to when they seek fresh goals or face new challenges. I have written it not only for men and women who feel they need some help in achieving their goals, but also for young men and women just starting out in life who, I hope, will use it as a psychological road map that will lead them more easily and directly to their hearts' desires.

CHAPTER ONE

A Psychological Toolbox

Love, power, riches, success, a good marriage, exciting sex, fulfillment are not impossible dreams. They can be yours if you want them.

Psychologists have amassed a tremendous amount of information about people. What makes them angry, what frustrates them, what makes them coo with pleasure. We know a lot about how emotions affect thoughts and actions. We have information on what causes stress and we know how to use stress creatively. We have data on why some people succeed and why others do not.

Most psychologists use their knowledge to help people who are trapped in unhappy marriages, whose children are in trouble, who are depressed or lonely or grieving, who need help to go on living. This, of course, is as it should be. We are members of a helping profession. But psychological findings can also—and should —be used to enrich the lives of people who are healthy and vibrant, to make their lives even more joyful, to help them get what they want out of life. And that is the purpose of this book.

In the following pages, I outline key psychological findings and techniques and explain how you can use them to attain your own goals. I think of this book as a kind of psychological toolbox to be used by men and women who want to get the most out of life. There is nothing esoteric about the techniques that I recommend. They are scientifically based, absolutely straightforward, and as uncomplicated as I can make them. There are no gimmicks here. I've tried not to make any false promises. You can put what you learn to work immediately. And you can use this knowledge to get whatever you want out of life.

CHAPTER TWO

All I Wanted Was a Cadillac

How success makes you taller. How I won The Sixty-four-Thousand-Dollar Question. *And how it changed my ideas about what I wanted out of life.*

When I was in the fourth grade, there were only three things I wanted out of life: the best marks in my class, a blue velvet dress with a white lace collar to wear to birthday parties, and to be the best roller skater on the block. By the time I was in high school, I wanted a lot more. My parents, both lawyers, encouraged me to aim high. At one point I announced that I had decided to be a nurse when I grew up. "A nurse!" my mother said in disbelief. "Why not be a doctor?" Why not indeed?

And I did become a doctor—a psychologist and Doctor of Philosophy, not of medicine (I married one of those). Like most girls at that time, I wanted a happy marriage and a family more than anything else. I was fortunate enough to marry a wonderful man, a husband who is as pleased over my successes as he is over his own, even after more than a quarter of a century of

3

marriage. Our daughter, Lisa, has grown up to be a woman I respect—and my very good friend as well. And I have a career that allows me to do what I enjoy most in the world: help people understand themselves better.

Some people tell me that I'm lucky, but I shake my head. I don't believe in luck. We make our own good fortune.

It certainly was not luck that helped me win *The $64,000 Question*—something that gave a whole new direction to my life. At the time, I wanted a Cadillac more than anything else in the world. Milt and I used to sit in front of our television set every Tuesday night watching *The $64,000 Question*, the most popular program of the era. What does anyone do with $64,000? we asked each other. What must it feel like to be rich beyond belief?

We were poor. Two years out of medical school, Milt was earning $50 a month (it went a lot further in those days) as a resident. And I was not earning a penny. I had stopped teaching when Lisa was born. We were barely making ends meet and would not have managed to introduce those ends to each other if our folks had not helped us out.

By the time Lisa was three, I had had enough of being at home full time and was practically climbing the walls. I began looking around for work, but all the time I was applying for teaching positions and research grants, I kept thinking about *The Sixty-Four*. Why couldn't I get on that quiz show? And earn some of that wonderful money? I certainly could do as well as most of the contestants we had watched. It seemed reasonable that I, who had always been a good student, would be able to make it to the Cadillac level. I had it all figured out. After I won the Cadillac, Milt and I would ride around in it for a couple weeks and show off to our friends; then we would sell it. There would be enough money to pay a baby-sitter for those times when I felt I just had to get out of the house.

But how to get on the show? Hundreds and hundreds of would-be contestants applied every week. Milt and I set to work to analyze the contestants and their fields of expertise. It did not take long tó realize that there was something paradoxical about each one—the shoemaker who had an encyclopedic knowledge of grand opera; the rough, tough Marine who was a gourmet cook. The producers of the show were obviously looking for a built-in incongruity, a paradox.

Well, I was a woman and a psychologist and short and blond, and that was psychologically incongruous, but one would have had to be another psychologist to appreciate the incongruity. It is based on the fact that people tend to see a person who has a title—doctor, professor, senator, or whatever—as a little bigger than life. In an experiment that has often been duplicated, one man spoke before three different groups. To the first group, he was introduced as a medical student; to the second, as a physician in general practice; and to the third, as Professor X, chief of the cardiology department of a great hospital. Afterward, the members of each group were given a quiz that was designed, they were told, to measure their comprehension and observation. One question asked was—how tall was the speaker? The majority of the group who believed him to be a medical student thought him shorter than those who believed he was a general practitioner. And those who thought they had been addressed by Professor X considered him even taller than the group that thought he was a general practitioner.

Tall people really do have an advantage. Tall men, for instance, get starting salaries that average out to be 12 percent higher than those given men of normal height. Women prefer tall men to short men. The tall person is considered more intelligent and more capable.

Height creates a halo effect; it may or may not be consistent with the facts, but it helps. (See Chapter Seven for an explanation of how the halo effect works.)

When I was introduced to strangers as Dr. Brothers, I had come to expect them to do a double double take. First, because I was a woman. Second, because I was short. Even today people are often surprised when they meet me. One woman recently accused me of being an impostor. The real Joyce Brothers, she told me, was nearly six feet tall. The title conjured up a picture of physical stature in her mind, a picture that she could not reconcile with the reality.

But I could not expect a letter of application setting forth my qualifications as *Psychologist: short, female, blond* to be taken seriously. I had to have something more, a specialty that was incongruous with my appearance and my profession. But what? I went through the Yellow Pages trying to find a sufficiently exotic interest or occupation. I considered becoming an amateur (and strictly legal) safecracker. Or a chimney sweep. I made list after list of odd occupations. Finally I narrowed down the choice to plumbing and boxing. No one would expect a female psychologist to be an expert on either. Milt advised me to choose boxing. It was sexier, he said. A blonde who knew all about knockouts had more appeal than one who specialized in stopped-up toilets.

And so I went to work to become an expert on the manly art. I ate, drank, and slept boxing. I even borrowed a series of films on the great fights of the century and rented a projector so I could run them off at home. When Milt came home at night, we watched the boxing films; then he would pick up a sports magazine or a book of boxing statistics and shoot questions at me.

There were times when I felt that I had made a terrible mistake. If anyone had offered me ten dollars, I would gladly have given up the whole idea. Ten dollars? Ten cents would have done it. But nobody offered. I would wake up in the middle of the night and ask myself what in the world I was doing.

Finally I felt confident enough to apply and sent off a letter describing myself as a psychologist and an expert on boxing. I also enclosed a snapshot, the fluffiest, blondest picture of myself I had.

Two days later, while I was washing my hair, the telephone rang. It was Western Union. A telegram was read to me. The producers of *The $64,000 Question* wanted me to call immediately. I wrapped a towel around my head and dialed.

"Are you really a boxing expert?" they asked.

"I'm an expert on boxing statistics," I said.

"Can you come down to the studio?"

"Oh, yes. When?"

"Right now."

"I can't," I wailed. "I've just washed my hair. It's all wet."

"Tie a kerchief over it," they said. "Take a cab and come right down. We'll pay for the cab."

I ran a comb through my wet hair, tied a kerchief over my head, woke up Lisa from her nap, and rushed down to Rockefeller Center with my cranky, sleepy three-year-old. I was asked a few questions. And then—"Okay," the man said. "You're going on." And two weeks later I was on *The Sixty-four*.

I kept going on and on and on. I passed the goal I had originally set for myself, that Cadillac. And then one night I won. Won *The Sixty-four!*

This was a watershed experience for me, the first time I had gone all out, giving up everything else in my life to get what I wanted. And it changed the whole direction of my life. I knew what it was to work and work hard, but I had never worked so intensely before, never had this kind of total commitment. I had pushed my energies and my brain and my emotions to the limit, to the point where it hurt—and it paid off. In so many ways. I was asked to appear on radio and television shows, to lecture, to write. And I took to it the way a duck takes to water.

Earlier I had been looking forward to reentering the academic world, but now I found myself thinking that my only audiences there would be my students, and my only readers those colleagues who subscribed to the professional journals where I hoped I would be publishing research findings from time to time. And here was this beguiling, exciting world of radio and television, of large audiences. Did I still want to bury myself in the laboratory and the classroom?

There was no question about what I wanted. I wanted to be part of this new world. I could teach, only now there would be no limit to the number of people I could reach as a psychological journalist. I would have the potentially largest classroom in the world—the whole radio and television audience. I could translate the results of psychological research into everyday terms that people could apply to their own lives.

Six months earlier, I had thought I wanted a Cadillac more than anything else in the world. Now I knew better. I wanted the fame and fun and money of this new-to-me world of mass communications. And now I understood that I could use my knowledge of psychology, of people's reactions and interactions, motivations and needs to help me get what I wanted. And I did. You can too.

I do not mean to set myself up as a textbook example of success. Like everyone else, I have experienced failure—and tried to learn from it. I tell this story because this experience was the chief source of my interest in how people get what they want out of life—and how they determine just what it is they want. Over the years, I have observed people who have solid, happy marriages, people who manage vast enterprises, people who perform pioneering surgery, people who have become very rich, who are world-famous, and people who lead quiet, happy lives. I have followed the research on motivation and manipulation, on energy levels and degrees of commitment. I have advised large corporations how to get what they want and schoolchildren on how to to get what *they* want. And I have come to the conclusion that the person who truly knows what he or she wants out of life and who is willing to work for it will achieve that goal. The first—and most important—step is to find out what you really want. Not what you think you should or what someone else thinks you should, but what you, the inner you, really wants out of life.

CHAPTER THREE

Money Isn't Everything — Honestly

Is it money or sex you really want? Or excitement? Or love? Or status? Reaching the point at which money no longer buys happiness. The best years of marriage. The primitive needs that rule our lives without our knowledge. What we can learn from the mice in the sandbox. And how some people fall into the Secondary Gain Trap.

When we talk about what we want most out of life, we are really talking about happiness. What will make me happy? What do I find most satisfying? What do I need to feel fulfilled?

These can be the hardest questions in the world—especially since happiness is always a by-product, never a goal. The person who sets out to seek happiness never finds it. So most of us are somewhat confused about what we really want. Our values and goals change as we change and as the society in which we live changes. And there are forces at work in our unconscious that can distort our desires. Because of these subterranean forces, most people will say—some cynically but most quite sincerely—that all they need to make them happy is money. A lot of money.

"Victor and I would get along like turtledoves," Deirdre said, "if only we had enough money. But we don't. We fight about money all the time."

"It's impossible to satisfy her," Victor complained. "She always wants more. It would take a million dollars to please her. I only wish I had it to give her. Honest to God, I think I'd give my right arm for a million dollars."

"If we had a million dollars," Deirdre said, a dreamy look in her eyes, "our marriage would be perfect."

These two were not fighting about money at all. They were fighting about sex. Deirdre felt cheated by Victor's twice-a-week, once-over-lightly lovemaking. And Victor felt threatened by what he considered Deirdre's ravening sexual appetite. He would roll off, sated and half asleep, only to have his wife snuggle closer and try to arouse him again—usually without success; whereupon Deirdre would flounce into the bathroom and clatter around, grumbling loudly that Victor thought only of himself.

Victor's reaction—a way of asserting his mastery—was to tighten the purse strings, making Deirdre account for every last penny she spent. Deirdre retaliated with her credit cards, running up bills that triggered more money fights.

It did not take a million dollars to satisfy Deirdre. It took two weeks of work with a therapist who helped the couple establish a mutually rewarding sexual relationship. Both Deirdre and Victor agree that they are much happier now—and that money plays no significant role in their present state of marital bliss.

Mario, an insurance salesman, who describes himself as a swinging sophisticate, has a deskful of overdue bills and a blood pressure reading of 190 over 110. His doctor recommended diet and exercise. "If that doesn't bring it down, we'll try medication," he said.

Mario shook his head. "The only thing that will help me is money. Give me another twenty thousand dollars a year and I won't ask anything more out of life. I'll be able to relax, and that will bring my blood pressure down."

His new sports car; his custom-made English suits; his beach house at Malibu, where he throws frequent parties to show off his "starlet of the week," are all part of his efforts to gain admiration and establish his status in the eyes of others, to conceal his feelings of inadequacy from the world—and especially from himself.

Deirdre and Victor were wrong. Mario was wrong. And I was wrong in thinking that the money represented by the Cadillac prize on *The Sixty-four* was what I wanted more than anything else in the world. Deirdre and Victor wanted a good sex life. Mario wanted status, to have people think highly of him. And I wanted more excitement in my life. Not money. I was bored. I wanted to be part of the world instead of being tucked away in a tiny apartment with a baby day in and day out.

The all-I-need-to-be-happy-is-money belief is baloney. Two of the richest women in this country, Gloria Vanderbilt and Charlotte Ford, have turned their backs on lives of luxurious leisure and privilege to work long, hard days, often six and seven days a week. Gloria Vanderbilt pyramided her artistic talent into an extremely successful career designing fabrics, china, and clothes. Her designs are sought after by big manufacturers and displayed in department stores and specialty shops all over the country. And Charlotte Ford, daughter of Henry Ford, rich in her own right and married to a rich man, has created a highly regarded line of women's fashions.

When asked why she gave up her freedom to work in the heart of New York's grimy and far-from-glamorous garment district, Charlotte said, "Getting up in the morning and having something to do is terrific. I made a decision to do something with my life instead of sitting home being bored."

These are not rich women dabbling dilettante style. They are passionately involved in creativity and in the dollars-and-cents world of business. But not just for the money, except in the sense that money symbolizes achievement. For self-actualization. For fulfillment. In the same way that millions of women juggle their many-faceted lives as mother, wife, housekeeper, and working woman. No money could make up for the fatigue, for the constant pressure of too much to do and not enough time to do it in. No, there is more to it than that. These women, almost all of them, are doing what they really want to do, getting what they want out of life—and it's not just money.

Men also demonstrate time after time that money is not what they want most out of life. Offhand, I can think of three men I know well who have given up highly paid positions or the chance to advance into high-ly paid positions to do what they want.

I think of Mac, a public relations man whose yearly income was in the six-figure bracket. Mac moved to Rhode Island two years ago. His children go to public schools now instead of private schools, and they live in a winterized beach house instead of a splendid suburban mansion. Mac now spends half the year operating a charter fishing boat and the other half of the year doing free-lance work, taking on only those projects which appeal to him. He earns less than a fifth of what he used to earn, but he assures me that he has never been happier.

"I get the same kind of kicks out of my charter fishing operation," he said, "that I used to get out of landing those big contracts to handle political campaigns. And no ulcers," he added.

Money honestly is not everything. The Greeks had a myth for it that most of us read in school. When Dionysus asked King Midas what he wanted more than anything else in the world, Midas replied without the slightest hesitation, "Pray grant that all I touch be turned into gold."

And Dionysus granted his wish.

Midas hastened to put his new power to the test. He reached up and plucked a leaf from a tree—and it turned to gold in his hand. He bent down and picked up a pebble—and it turned to gold in his hand.

"I am the richest man in the world, the happiest man in the world!" he marveled.

When he reached home, he ordered his servants to prepare a feast. "I am hungry and thirsty," he said. But the wine turned to gold at his lips, and the bread turned to gold before he could get his teeth into it. And as he reached out to his daughter in dismay, she too turned into gold.

And Midas cursed himself for having been so stupid.

But we do not need to go back to the myths to understand the hollow promises of money. In the eighteenth century, Sir John Sinclair wrote that the gathering of facts and figures on personal incomes and possessions was the best way of ascertaining the "quantum of happiness" enjoyed by a country's inhabitants. Almost two centuries later, however, Dr. Angus Campbell of the University of Michigan had to disagree with the eighteenth-century statistician.

"We produce a flood of statistics that relate to the material aspects of American life," Dr. Campbell said, "to income, expenditures, and savings. If it is true that these data indicate the quantum of happiness enjoyed by Americans, it is quite clear that we have been defining happiness in monetary terms." And, he added, time has shown that this is a mistake. "Over the past three decades," he said, "this country has experienced an unprecedented rise in national affluence, a spectacular increase in average family income. We have also seen a phenomenal rise in crime, an epidemic of public violence, a greatly increased use of drugs, a continuing increase in the number of fragmented families. The gross national product is clearly not the touchstone against which the quantum of happiness can be assessed."

Study after study has shown that money is not the key to happiness—and has never been the key. In a recent survey of 52,000 men and women, most of whom were in the upper economic brackets, money, for married women, ranked thirteen out of sixteen possible sources of happiness, a finding that backs up Dr. Campbell's conclusions. With married men, money ranked tenth as a source of happiness; it was ninth with single women and seventh with single men.

"Money has never been a problem for me," said one study participant, "but I would change lives with anyone who has a decent sex life."

"I am now absolutely broke," a woman reported, "but much happier than I ever was married to a multimillionaire's son. My marriage was painful and unfulfilling. And though there was plenty of money, it was unbearable. I have no desire to be rich again. I am richer now in my love than I ever could be in cash."

A best-selling novelist who was among those taking part in the survey said, "I wish I were not devoted to acquiring money as the ultimate goal in life. I'm boxed in with a family and children to support. Everything I do is just to get more and more money to pay more and more bills. At one time, I could hold other ultimate values. Now I can't. Every time I try to care about a spiritual matter, I have to bust my ass earning more money."

And so the responses went. The message seems clear. Money is not synonymous with happiness. But—other studies show that people with higher incomes are happier than people with lower incomes. And these studies have been equally scrupulously carried out by qualified researchers.

Who is right? Who is wrong?

The truth is that both are correct. And this is not as contradictory as it would seem. Money can buy happiness, *but only up to a point.* And then the process either comes to a standstill or reverses itself.

We are miserable if we're cold and hungry because we cannot pay the fuel bill or buy food, if we can't pay the rent or buy shoes for the children. And when we find a job or get a raise and can buy warmth and food and peace of mind, can give our children the things they need, we are happy. But as soon as our income reaches the point at which we have some discretionary funds, money left over after we have provided for the necessities, the happiness increments are smaller and smaller.

Most couples, when they look back, discover that the early years when they were struggling to establish themselves, to get ahead at work, to cope with the babies, to balance an almost invisible budget were the best of all, the very happiest time. The later years may be fulfilling and happy, but they seldom equal the joy of those first struggling years when there was lots of love and very little money. Wise couples, who want to keep their marriages alive and satisfying in the middle and late years, will make a point of finding other struggles to share— but more about that in Chapter Twenty.

There is no question that people with an income of, say, $20,000 a year are happier than those with $10,000—and much happier than those with $5,000. But—most people will be no happier with $100,000 than with $20,000. They will be more comfortable, better dressed; live better; but they will not be significantly happier. The man or woman earning $20,000 a year will probably raise an eyebrow at this, but the facts are that a modestly adequate income *does* make for happiness and that great sums of money rarely do.

There is a reason why a modestly adequate income goes hand in hand with more solid happiness. Few people are aware that our primary goals are programmed into us, part of our genetic heritage. Psychologists call them prepotent needs. Until these needs are filled, we cannot fulfill ourselves, cannot set higher goals for ourselves, decide to become nuclear scientists, run for President, invent a better mousetrap. The prepotent needs have priority. They are survival needs: air, mothering, water, food, and sex. In that order.

"I don't believe it," said the chairman of the board of a large company. I had just explained that he could not expect people to buy his luxury products until their basic needs had been met. And I had told him that these security needs were very closely related to the prepotent needs I have just listed.

"What don't you believe?" I asked him.

"That order of needs that you just cited," he said. "You can't mean that sex ranks fifth in a list of human needs."

"I do indeed," I said, and I told him about the landmark study by which researchers determined the relative importance of these prepotent needs. The mechanics of it were remarkably simple, and it has been repeated by generations of psychology students.

A rat is put into a metal box that is separated from another box, which is called the goal box, by an electrified grid. If the rat is hungry when placed in his box, food is put in the goal box. If he is thirsty, water is in the goal box. If the rat has just given birth, her pups will be in the goal box. In other parts of the experiment, air is removed from the rat's box but not from the goal box. If the sexual drive is being tested, a female in heat is in one box and a male in the other. The number and intensity of shocks that the rat will sustain in its mad scramble to get to that other box containing the food or whatever are measured carefully.

Rats repeatedly sustained the strongest shocks for the greatest number of times to get to the box with air. They were willing to undergo almost as many shocks to get to the baby rats. (Even male rats, when given hormone injections, displayed this prepotent mothering need.)

Not every finding based on animal research is equally valid for humans, but the prepotent needs seem to be universal. They vary in strength from species to species. The lower down the genetic scale, the stronger and more instinctual they are. We can control our sex needs, for instance, but a male dog confronted with a bitch in heat has no control.

"I still don't understand," the chairman of the board persisted. "Why is the sexual need so low? After all, it's vital for the perpetuation of the species."

"More vital than air or food or water?" I asked. "People tend to think of sex as an all-powerful drive," I told him, "because in our culture sex is the only prepotent need that is not systematically satisfied.

"And what we don't have always seems more important than what we do have. We don't think about water until the pipes freeze and burst or the reservoir is polluted or the well runs dry, but we are very conscious of our sex needs, because sex is a scarcer commodity than some of the centerfold magazines would have us believe."

"You're telling me!" said the dignified chairman of the board.

The prepotent needs shape our lives and actions far more than we realize. If they are not met, the consequences can be devastating. A study released by the United States Congress in the early winter of 1976 revealed that a definite link existed, a cause-and-effect relationship, between unemployment on the one hand and murders, suicides, and deaths from stress-related illnesses on the other. During a period when a lot of people are out of work, there are more suicides, more homicides, more deaths caused by stroke and heart attacks.

People are not rats, and they do have self-esteem needs, so it would be an oversimplification to maintain that such a rise in deaths, illness, and violence is a direct consequence of the threat to the prepotent needs, but there is a link. Those needs are the genesis of our security needs. We need money for food, for clothing, for shelter. And most of us have to work to earn that money. When a man loses his job, the strain may become intolerable and result in suicide or illness.

So money becomes a substitute gratification in the equation of needs. If we need food, first we need money to buy that food. And for that reason, many people believe that money is what they want more than anything else. They don't. They want something more basic. They want to meet their prepotent needs, their security needs. Once these needs are met, people can go on to deal with their self-actualization needs—the psychologist's term for what they really want in life to fulfill their potential and make them happy. It is rarely money.

Money is a delusion. And it can also be a snare. A trap that will prevent you from reaching your most cherished goals. For most people, money is a means to an end, not an end in itself. And when you understand this distinction, then you are free to explore your dreams and desires, to decide what kind of life, what values, what goals you want for yourself.

But there are some people who say, "Yes, I understand that. My inborn needs have been met. I have enough money to provide for myself and my family or to buy that house in the country I have always wanted. But now I want more. And what I want more than anything else in the world is more money. I want enormous bank accounts, blue-chip stocks, gilt-edged bonds, solid real estate investments. I want great wealth. The more money I have, the happier I am—and the more I want." (I will tell these people how to go about getting what they want in Chapters Twelve, Thirteen, and Fourteen.)

Who are these people? Some are singleminded, near-paranoid souls, as I shall explain; some are people who find the same kind of challenge and excitement in making money that others find in automobile racing or sailing or gambling; and many are men and women who started with another goal. They may have wanted to be good husbands or wives, have their names in lights on Broadway, be a beloved family doctor—but they fell into a trap. Like Lowell.

Lowell had not placed much importance on money. He and Alison had met at a commune near Colorado Springs one summer almost twenty years ago. They were flower children who had decided to live outside the money-oriented society of their parents, to make their own world of peace and understanding and meditation. But with the onset of the mountain winter, with its cruel winds and cold and snow, the commune broke up and its members drifted away.

Alison and Lowell went back home to Cincinnati, where they lived with Alison's parents and ate bean sprouts and yogurt and chocolate bars and pizza and waited for their baby to be born. They had decided to name it Night Star. But when Night Star arrived, Lowell and Alison reverted to type. Lowell got a job. Alison studied Spock. And Night Star was christened Anthea after Lowell's grandmother.

But the young couple assured themselves that they would never get caught up in the rat race. They had long, earnest conversations about "using the system" to earn enough money to move into their own place, enough money for a quiet life filled with meditation and music and simple pleasures. For Saturday-night suppers with friends when they would smoke a little grass, drink a little wine, and listen to Eastern ragas. Those were the dreams they shared. And Lowell was willing to work hard to make them come true.

He was promoted rapidly and began to earn good commissions on top of his salary. He enjoyed his work. "I never understood that work could be so absorbing," he told Alison. "Remember how I used to swear I'd never get caught in that nine-to-five routine? But it's not routine. It's a big adventure."

Lowell spent more and more time at the office or out with clients and less and less at home. Alison told herself, "Lowell is a good husband, a good father. And he works hard to give us a good life." And as the years went by they had a very good life. Not much meditation or listening to Indian music, and no grass except for the manicured lawn that surrounded their large house. No more Saturday suppers of brown rice and raw vegetables, but carefully thought-out dinners for eight or twelve with French wines.

Occasionally Alison told Lowell that it would be nice if they could spend a quiet weekend together with no guests and no bulging briefcase full of work. And Lowell would agree; but by Sunday night he was so restless and bored that she always regretted her suggestion. She realized that what Lowell wanted to do more than anything else in the world was work seven days a week, making more money than they could spend.

What happened to Lowell? Where did Alison go

wrong? Is it her fault that Lowell does not enjoy their luxurious home? Never spends time with her and Anthea? That he is no longer interested in sex? No longer cares much about anything except what goes on in his office downtown? Is there another woman?

No, there is no other woman, and this is not a soap-opera scenario. It is the story—the real-life story, only slightly disguised—of a man who fell into a trap, almost as if he had fallen into the toils of a wicked magician who transformed what Lowell had once considered the means to an end into the end itself.

When I was a student, I was fascinated by an experiment in which laboratory mice were placed in cages with several inches of sand on the bottom. There was plenty of water for the mice, but no food was visible. It was buried under a layer of sand. The mice smelled the food and started scrabbling away with their tiny paws to uncover it. Each day their food was buried just a trifle deeper, until the mice were digging several inches down to get their dinner.

Then the researchers stopped burying the food. They put it on top of the sand where it was clearly visible and easy for the mice to get at. And the mice ate it. But—they kept on digging. Those mice dug holes in the sand for the rest of their lives. They dug for the sake of digging. There was no longer any reason for them to dig. Their food was readily available on the surface. Digging is not a normal activity for a mouse. And yet these mice never stopped digging until they died.

This experiment illustrated the principle of Secondary Gain—the substitution of the means for the end. Just as the mice mindlessly scrabbled in the sand when there was no longer any need to do so, Lowell was obsessed by making more and more money. (See pages 33-34 to learn how to avoid the Secondary Gain Trap.)

Money is one of the most powerful symbols in our society. The way we feel about it and the way we use it reveal a great deal about out characters. It is easy to become confused about the role of money in one's life. Remember—it is a commodity, a means to an end. Not an end in itself, as it became for Lowell. It is also important to remember that money can mask our real desires, as it did with Victor and Deirdre and with Mario. Until you understand this, it may be impossible to decide just what you want out of life.

I trust that by now most of you realize that it is not money.

CHAPTER FOUR

The Quick List Technique

*Why college students should not worry if they
don't know what they want in life. Why
women should keep their future-options open
longer than men. How childhood scenarios
govern your adult life—and why they should
not. How the Quick List Technique puts you
in touch with your subconscious. How to use
the Quick List Technique and its variations.
How to avoid the Secondary Gain Trap.*

Before your dreams can come true, you have to have
those dreams. Some people stride right out toward
whatever it is they want in life, but others shuffle their
feet and never get started because they don't know what
they want—and don't know how to find out.

Keith introduced himself to me after I spoke at a careers seminar at his Florida college. "What about people
like me?" he asked. "I'm going to graduate in June, and
all I really want to do is goof off for a month. Sleep late
and go to the beach."

"Well, there's nothing wrong with that," I said. "It's
a good start."

He looked surprised.

"Goofing off?" he asked.

"Absolutely. This is transition time for you, a time to

shift your mental gears. A vacation is a fine idea. And when it's over, you're not going to have any real trouble finding a job. It may not be ideal, but it will give you a standard to judge other jobs by, a chance to think more realistically about the role you want work to play in your life—and, with luck, it will feed you and pay the rent. You can't ask much more from a first job."

When young people tell me they don't know what they want to do with their lives, I explain that they should concentrate on finding out about life first. Some people have to try several directions before they find the one that is right for them. There is nothing wrong about this. In fact, for women there is a lot that is right.

Most women will be happier and more successful if they keep their options open and don't lock themselves into a career or marriage or life-style too early. Even today, when women are well aware that they can choose almost any pursuit or combination of pursuits from motherhood to space exploration (medical and psychological tests have shown that women can withstand the rigors of space as well as men), too often they play out crippling life scripts that do not reflect their capabilities or potential, but simply childhood expectations.

Little boys were told in a recent study that "A boy can be all sorts of things when he grows up. What would *you* like to be?" They wanted to be doctors and pilots and athletes and firemen—all the traditional roles that little boys have always wanted to fill.

Little girls were also told, "A girl can be all sorts of things when she grows up. What would you like to be?" The girls wanted to be nurses and teachers and mommies—also traditional roles. Their choices did not reflect the scope and diversity of the opportunities open to women today. The little girls had already absorbed the idea that boys became doctors and girls became nurses, despite the fact that the opposite is often true these days. They had started writing their life scripts casting themselves in subordinate positions.

Women should be aware of the sneaky power of these early scenarios and be prepared to revise them as one of my daughter's classmates did.

"People keep asking me what I want to do," Jennifer told me a few years ago. "And I don't know. I used to think I wanted to teach, but I don't. I'm majoring in economics, so I tell them that I want to be an economist, but that doesn't really mean anything. I suppose I'll end up being a secretary or something like that."

"I'd stop fretting," I said. "Right now your job is to do just what you're doing—learning, exploring new ideas, finding out about yourself and the world. You have plenty of time. When people ask you what you're going to do, just tell them that you haven't made up your mind yet and that you intend to take your time about it. Remember, you can do anything you really want to do. If you want to be a secretary, fine. That can be a very rewarding job. But you may discover that you prefer to *have* a secretary rather than *be* a secretary."

I am not alone in advising young people to take their time. Some of the hardest-headed men in the country agree with me. A survey of 30 top California executives, all of them men in charge of multimillion-dollar organizations, revealed that most of them did not believe in setting goals too early—especially not during the college years. They emphasized that college was the time for what one called "the mind-stretching exercises of the learning process." Another advised, "Taste everything on the table; then follow up on what interests you." They felt strongly about this, because all of them agreed that once a young person decided he or she wanted to get to the top in business or a profession, there would be very little time for dabbling in other interests. "To succeed in business demands sacrifice and total dedication to the job and the company," one president said. (See Chapter Eight, The Seduction of Total Commitment.)

It is not only young people who are bewildered. Men and women of all ages are searching for more rewarding life-styles. Today, perhaps for the first time in history, people believe that it is possible to get what they want. If they can decide what it is that they want.

When men and women over thirty tell me they don't know what they want out of life, I tell them they know more than they suspect. Unlike the Keiths and the Jennifers who have no experience to draw upon, these men and women have years of living behind them. They do not have to explore and experiment. Most mature individuals know exactly what they want out of life—on the subconscious level. The problem is in bringing this knowledge up to the conscious level.

It is not simply a job or a direction they are seeking. If it were, that would be easy. But our wants are much more complex. Chief among them are love, money, power, fame, success, friends, a good marriage, fine children, fun, sex, beauty, excitement, health, the respect of others, autonomy, and myriad combinations of these. The roles we choose in life are only one facet of what we want. We do not want to be chairman of the Community Chest, but to achieve status. Nor to be a model housewife, but to rear happy, healthy children who will grow up to be responsible, loving adults. Nor to be president of the United Whatever Corporation, but to be successful and wealthy.

One woman may want a good husband who can give her a comfortable life; another may want to be elected to Congress. The first wants love and money; the second wants power—but both want status and success. One man may want to have a large family and to be involved with the community; another may want to devote his time and energies to scientific research and want only minimal family and social obligations. The first seeks love, friends, a good marriage, fun, fine children, the respect of others; the second seeks fame, autonomy, the excitement of discovery. Money and power play no role in their lives.

These very brief examples demonstrate how complicated our desires really are and why it is difficult for some people to know just what it is they want. I have developed a technique that helps most people pinpoint just what they want most, that will make their lives most rewarding, in a very short time. I call it the Quick List Technique.

It helped Norman, who was pushing forty. He represented a drug concern and made the rounds of doctors' offices telling them about new medicines and leaving samples. He was a good salesman and made a good living, but this was no longer enough.

"I don't want to spend the rest of my life telling doctors about contraceptives and suppositories," he said. "If I don't make a change pretty soon, I'll be dragging this sample case around until I drop. But I'm damned if I know what I want to do instead."

"I suspect you know just what you want," I said. "And I think I can prove it to you."

I gave him a piece of paper and a pencil. "I'm going to ask you to make a list," I said. "The minute I say 'Go,' I want you to start writing. Don't stop to think. Just put down what comes into your head as fast as you can. Ready?"

"Ready," he said.

"Write down the three things you want most at this very moment. Go!"

When he finished, he pushed the paper over to me.

"I want a private office," I read, "well furnished, with a secretary outside the door. I want people to take me seriously and ask my opinion. I want a Jaguar sports car."

Norman looked a little sheepish, embarrassed. "Dreams of glory," he said self-mockingly.

"Not at all," I told him. "What this list shows is that you want success and the good things that success brings. You want recognition of that success. And a degree of power. You want to stop traveling around, to be an executive instead of a salesman."

I paused. "What I'm telling you is nothing new, is it? You knew all this before you made the list."

He nodded. "I guess I did. I keep thinking, though— as long as I'm selling, no one at the head office is ever going to see me as anything except a salesman. And that's never going to get me into the management track."

We discussed this. Was there something he could do about it? Could he tell his boss that he felt he was ready to take on executive responsibilities? Did he have any ideas of how the company could improve its procedures? Make more money? Or expand? Was there anything Norman had learned from his selling career that would benefit the company?

It turned out that Norman had given a lot of thought to the more effective use of advertising. "The company does those expensive institutional ads in business magazines and it advertises new products in the medical journals, but doctors are so busy, they often don't read the medical journals they subscribe to. That's a lot of advertising going to waste. My idea is to do more direct-mail advertising. Make it very personal. Direct to the doctor telling him about new developments, new products. Then when our representative calls, the physician is halfway sold.

"And then," Norman continued, "I am convinced that we should put out a kind of directory to our products. Something the physician can use for easy reference. Before he prescribes medication, he can look it up quickly, check the side effects and the contraindications. Drugs are so complicated these days, doctors can't keep it all in their heads. And they may not have our leaflets on that particular medication handy."

This sounded like very good thinking to me. "What have you done about these ideas?" I asked.

"Nothing," he said. He looked at me. "I've just realized that I should stop waiting for something to happen. It's up to me to make things happen. To take that first step. Why couldn't I figure that out for myself?"

"You would have eventually," I told him. "You see, you knew just what you wanted all the time. But now let's talk about that sports car. If you really want it that much, why don't you buy one? You can afford it. What's stopping you?"

He laughed. "I guess I just can't permit myself to get what I want. It's part of the same pattern, isn't it?"

A couple of days later Norman called to announce that he now owned a metallic silver sports car with red leather upholstery. And two years later, he called me to say that he was opening his own business as an advertising consultant. His firm had welcomed his ideas. And the ideas had worked. Word had gotten around, and soon other people were asking him to advise them on a free-lance basis. Eventually the demand was enough to warrant his going into business for himself.

Once Norman was able to articulate what he wanted, he was able to go after it and get it.

It is often very difficult to see the obvious. That is why this Quick List Technique is so helpful. When people think about what they want most in life, they tend to think in vague, amorphous terms. But a wish is specific. And a list is concrete. It is here and now. There is nothing vague about wanting a private office with a secretary sitting outside the door. Or about wanting people to recognize your expertise and pay you for it. By the time a person has written down the three things he wants more than anything else at a given moment, written them down as fast as he can without conscious thought, a pattern usually begins to emerge.

Anyone can use this technique. You need no special training.

The Quick List Technique is deceptively simple. Deceptive because it is so easy and so fast that it is difficult to see it as the powerful psychological tool it is. This technique is a way of revealing a person's unconscious and subconscious desires to himself rapidly—and harmlessly. Some psychological techniques are emotional dynamite and should never be used except with a psychologist or psychiatrist who is highly skilled in understanding people's reactions and can defuse the dynamite when necessary. But the list technique is constructive, never destructive. There is something about being told or telling yourself to write down your thoughts or desires very quickly that seems to disarm the inner censor. The censor lets down its guard, and in seconds or minutes you can discover things about yourself that you may never have suspected. But the censor is never completely disarmed. It prevents you from revealing thoughts that might be too troubling for you to cope with. For these reasons, I feel this is the ideal self-diagnostic technique.

Before reading any further, get a piece of paper and a pencil. Now, quickly, write down the three things you want most in the world at this very moment. Don't stop to think. Just scribble your wishes down on that piece of paper.

Now read what you have written. Have you learned anything about yourself? Whether the answer is yes or no, or whether or not you know what you want out of life, I would like to suggest that you pursue this Quick

List Technique for six to eight weeks. You will learn something about yourself.

Put this list away in your desk or bureau drawer or some convenient hidey-hole. Set aside two minutes a week for the next six to eight weeks to write your Quick List. It is best if the two minutes are on the same day of the week at about the same time of day. Any time that is convenient for you. Any time when you can be alone. Go to the bathroom to write if that is the only privacy you can arrange. And then, write down your three wishes just as fast as you can. Read what you have written, and then file the list away with the first list. At the end of six or eight weeks, take out all the lists and study them.

There will be a pattern. If you did not know what you wanted most in the world, you will have a clearer idea now. You will see a path to follow. And if you knew before you started what you wanted, you may discover that you have become more ambitious in your desires and more confident of achieving them. I want to caution you against making hasty decisions. Do not feel that the changes you want in your life can be accomplished overnight. There are dangers inherent in moving too fast in making any life change. Let the changes come naturally, little by little.

Most people will not need to use this technique, because they know what it is they want. Their desires may change from time to time, but they are aware of the changes. But if you are confused about what you want out of life, try it. It will give you a clearer view of yourself and your desires—and your needs.

There is another important use for this technique. And that is to help you avoid the Secondary Gain Trap. If you use the Quick List Technique every three or four months, you will be alerted to subtle changes in your goals. And when you spot such changes, it is important to ask yourself if you have lost sight of what you really want. Consider this seriously. Don't just say, "Oh, I'm doing as well as can be expected" or "It was a crazy idea. I should forget it." Don't let yourself down. Think about what has changed.

It may be that you have truly changed your goal, that the change reflects personal growth and achievement. But if you suspect that you are stuck on the psychological treadmill of the Secondary Gain Trap, this is the time to reassess your situation. Is this what you really want? Why did you change your tactics?

If you are confused, not sure that you know the answers to these questions, this is a good time to experiment with variations on the Quick List Technique. The following three variations can help you solidify your ideas about your goals and your future. Using the same technique, write, without stopping to think—

1. The names of the three people you admire most.
2. The names of the three people you would most like to be or be like.
3. The three nicest things anyone ever said about you.

And then try the Quickest Lists of all. Are you ready? Write down—

1. The happiest day of your life.
2. The most miserable day of your life.
3. The person you feel closest to.
4. The accomplishment you are proudest of.

Tell the truth. These lists are for your eyes only. Read over what you have scribbled down and think about what your lists tell about you. They may seem simple, but they reveal your values and your aspirations.

Now put them away for a couple of weeks. When you take them out and reread them, ask yourself, if you were writing these lists today, would they be the same? Or would you make some changes? Cross out the items you no longer agree with and write in the changes. Now think about your lists in terms of your goals and your future. Have you chosen an appropriate goal for the person revealed by these lists? A woman whose most-valued accomplishments all involve a competitive element, a joy in winning, is not going to be happy pursuing a nurturing goal, whether that of mother, teacher, or therapist.

Men and women with potential have many goals, and these goals shift from time to time. Don't feel that you are locked into working for something just because you decided a year ago that that was what you wanted. If you want to change course, go ahead. Change. Just be sure that you are the one in charge of your life. That you are not emulating those mice endlessly digging in the sand.

CHAPTER FIVE

Do You Have What It Takes to Succeed in Business?

The simple test that measures your success potential. Why you need a friend or spouse to read page 247 for you.

You have set your goal. You want to succeed in business.

Is this a realistic goal? Does it reflect what the inner you really wants? Have you got what it takes to succeed?

You can find out. It is possible to test your success potential. Harvard psychologist David McLelland and other scientists have discovered that there is one personality characteristic which seems to be the true key to success. They call it Motive A. And they have developed a test that can disclose immediately whether or not you possess this characteristic.

If you want to succeed in business, take this test. It is simplicity itself. I have not included it in this short chapter because once you know what it is, it *can't* help you find out whether you have that essential quality. So please hand this book to your spouse or a friend and ask him or her to arrange for you to take the test. The person you choose will find the instructions on page 247.

All you need to know at this point is that it involves a group of people. It is theoretically possible to take the test by yourself, but the findings will not be as reliable as if you took it with other people. Invite some friends over for drinks or dinner or an evening of bridge or whatever and then ask them if they are willing to participate in the test. It takes only a few minutes. Your friend or spouse will be able to tell you whether you possess Motive A immediately after you take the test, and I will tell you about Motive A and what it means in Chapter Ten.

Please try to contain your curiosity and do not turn to page 247 or read Chapter Ten until you have taken the test. You will be the loser if you give in to your curiosity—because, as I have explained, the test will no longer be valid.

CHAPTER SIX

Learning What You Need to Know

What you can learn from Pavlov's dog. How to get rid of tension buildup in less than sixty seconds. Are you a lark or an owl? How to discover your brain's peak working time. The best temperature for learning. Soundproof your study for less than a dollar. The five-step learning technique. The Catch-22 of learning—and how to get around it. The echo that leads you astray. How a glass of milk can help you.

How to apply for a job,
How to advance from the mail room,
How to sit down at a desk,
How to dictate memoranda,
How to develop executive style . . .

This book is all that I need,
How to—*how to*—HOW TO SUCCEED!*

This was the opening song in that hit musical of the sixties, *How to Succeed in Business Without Really Trying.* And let me say right now that there is no way, absolutely no way of succeeding in business without really trying. Not even if you marry the boss's daughter (and it is even more difficult if you marry the boss's son—see Chapter Eleven). If you want to get to the top, you have to give it all you've got. And that is called Total Commitment (see Chapter Eight). But the young hero of *How to Succeed* etcetera, etcetera, intent on making it out of the mail room and into the executive suite, had the right idea. He had a book on how to succeed.

A how-to book can make all the difference. I learned that when I was eleven years old and very much interested in boys. But I didn't know how to talk to them. What did you say to a boy? I went to the library and took out a book on how to interest men. It was not written with an eleven-year-old in mind, I am sure, but it was helpful. The most useful piece of advice I gleaned was that you should make each man you spoke to at a party or a dance believe that all your attention was centered on him and that he was the most interesting man in the room. It worked then. And it works now.

All my life when I did not know how, I have looked for a book that told me how. For the last few years Milt and I have been restoring our tumbledown farmhouse, a how-to book in one hand and a hammer in the other. A book is not enough, of course. It is what you bring to the book; your ability to absorb the information it contains and make those facts, those insights, yours. If you know how to absorb information, you can do just about everything—start your own business, build a happy marriage, even shingle a roof.

Almost every goal we set for ourselves involves learning. The actress must learn her lines if she wants her name to be up in lights. The mountain climber must study the terrain and the weather if he expects to get to the top. The businessman must keep himself informed on a broad spectrum of information from corporate law to commodity markets. Most of this knowledge has to be acquired by study, book learning. Even sexual expertise should not be a matter of trial and error in the bedroom.

The ability to learn what you need to know in a hurry is the basic tool for getting what you want. Wispy Woody Allen types have become exciting sex partners because they knew how to learn what they needed to know. Office boys have become division chiefs, salesmen have become members of the board, secretaries have become corporate executives because they knew how to absorb vital information faster than the next person.

Some time ago I spoke before an association of young top executives in the Middle West. Afterward, a member of the board took me to the airport.

"I'm working on expanding my brainpower," he told me as we drove along the highway.

"Oh? That's interesting," I said. "How are you doing that?"

"I do mental exercises every morning," he said. "This morning, while I was jogging, I memorized the number of windows facing the street in each house on our block."

"What is the point of that?" I asked.

"To exercise my brain. To increase its capacity."

That ambitious young man was wrong. The brain is not like a muscle that, if you exercise it, will get more muscle tone so that you can pick up heavier objects or press down harder. You cannot learn how to use your brain better or add to your brainpower.

If you go out and memorize the number of windows in each house on your block or the number of dandelions on the lawn or the number of street lights between your house and the bus stop, it will improve your ability to memorize numbers of windows or dandelions or street lights. And that is all. It will not improve your ability to balance complicated accounts or help you cope with the metric system. Your ability to memorize cannot be transferred to help you learn to buy and sell stocks profitably or program a computer. It will not improve your IQ score.

Until a short time ago, educators and others believed that if you studied a difficult subject like calculus or ancient Greek, it would improve your thinking ability. It will not. It will increase your knowledge of calculus or ancient Greek. That is all. The uses of the mind are not transferable.

But you can learn how to learn faster and more effectively. And that can give you a significant edge over your rivals in the race to the top. Later on in this chapter, I am going to outline a technique that will help you assimilate information rapidly—the Five Step Learning Technique. While the uses of the mind are not transferable, techniques are. You can use the same technique to master the Tantric approach to sex, to learn how to handle puts and calls on Wall Street, to encourage people to do what you want them to.

When I was cramming my head full of boxing statistics for *The Sixty-four,* I used all the psychological know-how I had accumulated in my years of graduate study. Months later when the quiz-show scandals broke and some contestants were found to have had prior knowledge of the questions they were asked, I appeared before the grand jury charged with getting at the truth in each case. All kinds of questions about boxing were flung at me. They spent hours passing around boxing encyclopedias, opening them at random and quizzing me on the contents. I did not miss once. I passed with flying colors and head held honorably high.

The learning techniques I had devised for myself had worked.

Since that time I have added to those techniques and changed them as scientists discovered more about the learning process. I use these techniques constantly. Not only to absorb the information I need from the scores of research papers and scientific journals I study, but to learn (and sometimes I have only one or two days to do it) the management, marketing, and personnel policies of the corporations that retain me as a psychological consultant. My learning techniques have always worked for me, and they will work for you—*provided that you have taken the first, all-important psychological step that is the key to effective learning.*

If you do not take this step, all the psychological know-how in the world is useless.

If you *cannot* take this step, it is a strong indication that the inner you is not truly interested in the goal you have set. In that case, I suggest you review the material in the previous chapter and rethink just what it is you really want. Use the Quick List variations to help you discover just what the inner you does want.

What is this key to effective learning? It could not be simpler. *You must want this knowledge—really want it.*

We have all known people who hear only what they want to hear. The brain is even more selective than the ear. It learns what it wants to learn, no matter how complicated the subject, effectively and quickly, but it resists material it does not want to learn although that material may be primer-simple. This helps explain such exasperating memory lapses as that of the mathematician who can never remember which floor his mother-in-law lives on.

If you are convinced that you have a high need-to-know, if you honestly believe that this knowledge is going to help you get what you want, you will absorb it easily. If you approach the material in a spirit of dutiful drudgery, however, forget it. You will never master it properly.

So if the inner you is convinced that you have a need-to-know how to play backgammon or to understand zero-based accounting, here are psychological techniques that will help you learn faster and retain the information longer.

You will learn more and faster whether you are analyzing stock tables or studying the niceties of diplomatic etiquette if you settle down to work in the same room at the same desk at the same time every time you study. This helps you condition yourself to study in very much the same way that Pavlov taught his dog to salivate when it heard a bell.

What the Russian scientist did was ring a bell, then feed the dog. A dog's first natural response to food is to salivate. Every time Pavlov rang the bell and put a bowl of food in front of the dog, it salivated. After many, many repetitions, the dog associated the ringing with food, and when Pavlov rang the bell, the dog salivated—without seeing or smelling food. This is a learned response.

You, of course, will not start drooling at the prospect of studying; but you will learn to start work immediately when your bottom makes contact with the chair if you repeat the situation often enough. You will condition yourself to associate the time and place with acquiring new information, and it will become easier and easier to switch your attention to your work. You will waste less time sharpening pencils or filing your nails or writing out a check for the electric bill before getting down to work.

It is not always possible to provide oneself with ideal conditions. Busy men and women have to use whatever time they can find to assimilate the information they need. Many executives have material they want to learn recorded on tapes which they play in the car as they commute or in taxis as they go from one appointment to the next. One woman in the cosmetics industry studies business French under the dryer when she goes to the hairdresser in preparation for her semiannual trips to France.

It is harder to concentrate under these conditions; but you can use a Pavlovian device to help blot out distractions. What I do is get out whatever it is I have to do and say to myself, "I am going to concentrate on this now. I am going to think of nothing else." I always use the same words. This is an effective device. Since I shuttle between the East and West Coasts so often, I have conditioned myself to think of planes as an extension of my study with an added efficiency factor— no telephone calls to interrupt me. The minute I have buckled my safety belt, I get out my work and tell myself, "I am going to concentrate on this now." And I do everything that I would normally do in my own study. I have written most of this book on airplanes.

But everyone needs a primary study spot. It should contain a desk and a chair that supports your back, the kind that forces you to keep your feet on the floor and sit up straight. Learning is tiring, and your muscles, especially those in the back of your neck and in your shoulders, tense up and ache. The back-support chair keeps your body in proper alignment and staves off the aches and pains longer. If your muscles do tense up, take time to work out the tension. These four tension-dispellers take less than sixty seconds to do.

1. Stand up straight with your arms over your head and stretch up as high as you can. Then lean over and hang down limply. Don't try to touch your toes. Don't force yourself down. Just bounce gently, hanging loose, ten times. Then straighten up and stretch high again.
2. Drop your chin onto your chest and rotate your head slowly to the right two times and then to the left two times.
3. Place your fingers at the base of your skull at the

back of your neck. You'll feel an indentation there. Press down gently and pull out with your fingers, and move your fingers slowly down, pressing and pulling, as far down your backbone as you can reach.

4. Rotate your shoulders forward five times and backward five times.

And now get back to work.

Thinking is tiring—no matter whether you are trying to decipher an annual report, forecast next season's sales, or write a book—but your brain uses very little more energy when you think than when you are not thinking. No matter how difficult the problem you are trying to solve or the theory you are trying to understand, you burn no more than three or four extra calories an hour. This is why people do not lose weight from worry unless they stop eating. And you won't lose weight from studying either, and it is a mistake to provide yourself with a snack to munch on while you're working. You don't need it. You are not using that much energy. And, eating will interfere with your concentration.

Mental activity thrives in a chilly atmosphere, so keep the room on the cold side—60 to 65 degrees is most conducive to learning. Theater people are well aware of this chill factor. Some comedians insist on appearing in underheated theaters, and television studios are purposely kept cold because the audience responds faster and laughs more. A New York hostess, famous for the sparkling conversation at her dinner table, told me that in winter she opens the windows of her dining room, closing them just minutes before her guests sit down. In the summer she turns the air conditioning on full blast. "People are wittier when they are a little cold," she says.

Conversely, corporations have been known to turn up

the heat in the auditorium where the annual stockholders' meeting is held to keep hostile questions about profits and policies to a minimum. The hotter the room, the more lethargic the stockholders and the less embarrassing the questions shot at corporate executives.

Your study should be quiet. Most people find it difficult to concentrate when the television is on or the dog is barking or the street outside is being torn apart by jackhammers.

A couple of years ago when I had a daily question-and-answer radio program, a businessman called in.

"I've just had a big promotion," he said. "It means that I have to bring work home at night until I get on top of my new responsibilities. But I can't get anything done. The television is blaring away in the living room. The dishwasher is churning in the kitchen. The telephone rings incessantly. And the kids fool around and make a lot of noise. I can't expect everyone to tiptoe just because I have work to do, but even in my den with the door closed there is too much noise for me to concentrate."

I suggested that he stop at the drugstore on his way home and buy a box of wax ear stoppers. They cost about seventy-five cents. Not an enormous expenditure. If these did not filter out enough of the household hubbub, I told him to wear earmuffs as well. For days and days afterward, I had telephone calls and letters from other people who had been listening, thanking me for the idea.

Most people study in the evening after the day's work, but that may not be the best time for you. A junior executive in a corporation that had retained me as a consultant came into my office late one afternoon.

"How is your course going?" I asked her. The company was sending her to a seminar in management procedures. She was the first woman to be given the kind of management training that the firm had always given promising young male executives.

She made a face. "I think I'm flunking," she said. "That's why I'm here. I would really appreciate some advice. If I fail, it means no more promotion. It also means that it will be a long time before they give another woman a chance."

"What's the problem?" I asked.

"I can't find time to study," she said. "I'm at the university from nine until noon and at the office from one to six. There's a lot of reading and report writing involved in the course, but when I get home, well, Henry and I have a drink and relax for a while. Then I get dinner and we eat and I clean up the kitchen. And then I try to get down to work. But I'm so beat that I can't concentrate. By ten o'clock I've had it. And the thing is, I'm fascinated by the material. I'm suddenly seeing whole new vistas opening up. I want to do the work. But I just can't."

"You're probably a lark," I said, not bothering to ask whether Henry could not help with some of the chores so she could get to her homework earlier. I felt this was a case of out-of-sync body rhythms, not overwork.

"A lark?"

I explained that people are divided into larks and owls, depending on inborn body rhythms. "Your ability to concentrate and learn is affected by the changes in your daily temperature cycle. Most people's temperature is lowest around two in the morning, but some reach their low point at five or six in the morning, and others at eleven or twelve at night.

"Try getting up two hours earlier in the morning," I said. "See if you function better then. It would be a good idea if you monitored your temperature for a week to find out when it's highest. Take it when you get up in the morning and then about every three hours until bedtime. By the end of a week, you should have a good idea of when it's highest. And that's going to be the best time for you to study."

The next week she reported that her daily temperature high was around eleven in the morning, much earlier than most people's. And the early-bird study period had made a significant difference. "I'm accomplishing a lot more," she said.

Owls are just the opposite. They will do much better, learn more effectively and faster if they study in the evening.

No matter what it is you want to study or what facts you want to absorb—your management-procedures homework, a prospectus for a mutual fund, the feasibility of heating with solar energy, the ins and outs of a proposed tax shelter, or how to cast a horoscope—the process is the same.

Here is the way to use the Five Step Learning Technique. Get together the material you want to learn. Sit down at your desk in a cool, quiet room at your physiologically optimum time, if it is at all possible, and—

1. Get an overview. Spread out the material and skim it to get an idea of just what you have to do; then divide it up. You may decide that it will take two or three days to learn what you need to know, so look through the material for logical breaking points and divide it up.
2. Then divide the material you plan to learn during today's study session into three parts. Plan to spend most of your time on the second part. REASON: The easiest learning is always at the beginning. The second-easiest material to learn is at the end. The hardest-to-grasp is in the middle. So emphasize the middle, but don't neglect the beginning and end.

3. Read the first section. As you read, tell yourself that when you have finished you are going to cover up the report or close the book and recite to yourself what you have just learned.
4. Now cover up that report or close the book. REASON: We tend to be unconscious cheaters. Our peripheral vision is very sneaky. If you just push the material you have been studying to one side, you may pick up clues without knowing it.
5. Recite what you have learned. Out loud, not just in your mind. If there is time, recite it several times. REASON: This allows you to check what you really have learned, and it reinforces that learning.

If you have time, it is even better to write down what you have learned while you are reciting it. REASON: There is a direct relationship between your senses and your memory. The more ways your brain senses something, the better it remembers it. If you have time to read key passages out loud, that can help too.

Repeat steps 3, 4, and 5 with the remaining two sections.

WARNING: While it is tremendously helpful to repeat something out loud over and over again, beware of the echo. Learning takes place first in the outer layer of the brain; then it passes to the thalamus, the inner core of the brain. Repetition reinforces our learning and speeds the progress of the knowledge to the brain core. But it is important to leave a few seconds between the repetitions of material you are learning or the technique won't work. This is because we "hear" inaudible echoes—mind echoes. Almost everyone has been betrayed by mind echoes at one time or another. A common experience is to look up a telephone number and repeat it in your head as you dial. But the line is busy.

You hang up and start to dial again—and discover that you can't remember the number. You have to look it up again.

You can remember the number if you just keep it going in your head, repeating it over and over. But when you stop repeating it, you lose the number. You begin to lose it as you dial the last two digits, because you no longer are keeping it going in your head. The echo has disappeared.

So if you are repeating material that you want to learn, make sure that you pause for a few seconds between repetitions so that you will really learn it and not fool yourself by parroting the echo—the echo that will not be there when you need it.

In an emergency, you can speed up the learning process. If you have only one night to absorb all the information you need, you can emulate the college student on the night before his final exam and cram. Much of what you learn will not stick for more than twenty-four hours, but that twenty-four hours may be all that matters.

How do you go about this speedup in learning? First, figure out what you absolutely have to know. Then concentrate on learning that material. Set aside a block of time to work. Let us say that you give yourself five hours—from six until eleven at night. (Don't plan to stay up all night drinking coffee and working. You can learn effectively for only a certain amount of time; then new learning comes too slowly to be worth the effort.) Eat a light supper and start working at six using the Five Step Learning Technique. Stop work at eight-thirty for half an hour. This is to give yourself a breather so that you can go back and work almost as productively as you did at the beginning of the evening.

During this half hour, have a cup of decaffeinated coffee or weak tea or an apple, but no heavy snack.

And no alcohol. Do not telephone. Do not chat with your family. Do not watch television or listen to the radio.

Then get back to work. At eleven, close your books and files and get ready for bed. If you are hungry, drink a glass of milk. As I will explain very shortly, this will both help you sleep more soundly and help you retain more of what you have learned.

The reason for these strictures against talking and watching television and all the rest is to minimize your RPI—Retroactive and Proactive Inhibition. Retroactive and Proactive Inhibition are the terms psychologists use for the dynamics behind the fact that the more you know, the more your knowledge interferes with what you want to learn, and the more you learn, the more it interferes with what you already know. It is the Catch-22 of the learning process.

When you were little, let us say that you met a freckle-faced little girl named Wendy. The name Wendy immediately became attached in your mind to that particular little girl. When you heard the name Wendy, you thought of that little girl, saw her freckled face in your mind's eye, even though people may have been referring to another Wendy.

You grow up and over the years you meet ten or twenty other Wendys. Now when you hear the name Wendy, you rarely think of that first freckled-faced girl. The association of the name with the first Wendy has been weakened by all the other Wendys in your life. The more Wendys you know, the less clearly you remember them.

The way RPI works when you are trying to learn something is that the more similar the material you are trying to learn at one time, the more it interferes with your learning. If you are going over the prospectuses for three stock issues in one evening, the information you glean will be more difficult to retain than if you went over one prospectus and then read a book on how to play the horses. You will retain more of that one prospectus and the information on betting on horse races than you would of the three prospectuses.

If you read just one prospectus and then watched television before going to sleep, you would retain even more of what was in the prospectus.

And if you went straight to bed after reading the prospectus, you would remember still more.

Any activity you engage in after learning something will interfere with your retention. The best thing to do if you want to remember what you have just learned is go to bed when you finish, since sleeping represents the least possible amount of activity. And that is why that glass of milk is so useful. The amino acid in the milk is transformed into a natural tranquilizer in the body and helps you go straight to sleep without tossing and turning and thinking about one thousand and one unrelated items.

We are all confronted from time to time with having to learn something in a hurry. You may be going on a job interview where it is important that you be knowledgeable about a company's markets and affiliations. You may have a date with a rising young politician and want to make a good impression on her with your knowledge of protective tariffs or your opinions on the federalization of welfare. Your boss may ask you to represent him in a meeting dealing with a situation about which you have only the sketchiest information.

In any of these hypothetical cases you can create an excellent impression if you demonstrate a grasp of the pertinent subject. But if you don't, you run the risk of being branded as not-quite-with-it and of losing your opportunity to know that young politician better or to get that job or impress the management committee.

I am not exaggerating. It might not seem fair for you to be judged solely by the impression you make at an initial or significant encounter, but there is often no re-semblance between what should be and what is.

The man or woman who wants to succeed in business must be aware of the importance of the impression he or she makes at these key encounters. The time and ef-fort you spend on preparing for them are never wasted. The way you acquit yourself at these times governs whether or not you reach the top. These are the make-or-break moments. And I will explain exactly why they are make-or-break in the next chapter.

But one last bit of advice here. If you are already relatively successful or think you are so close to attain-ing your goal that none of this information on how to learn applies to you, think again. Top executives never stop learning. Not if they want to stay on top. For ex-ample, six chief executives of companies with sales ranging from $10 million to $35 million a year have been studying with a group of Harvard professors for the last few years, learning new theories of executive action, more effective problem-solving techniques, and ways to use these in their own corporate lives under varying conditions of stress.

It is difficult for such a high-power group to spare time from their businesses, but they consider the learn-ing process important enough to devote three to five fifteen-hour days to their semiannual sessions with the experts from Harvard plus several hours of study on their own every week. Over the four years, only one man has missed a session.

Learning is a lifelong process. Now that you know how to learn rapidly and effectively, you are several steps closer to your goal. These techniques will be among your most useful tools in getting what you want out of life.

CHAPTER SEVEN

How to Use Your Halo to Get What You Want

The crucial make-or-break movements. How the halo effect can work for—or against— you. Five rules for creating a positive halo. The listening technique that wins friends. How Chet's office created a successful halo effect for him. Why a beige raincoat is a male wardrobe must. Why businesswomen should wear suits. When clumsiness can create a good first impression. The pitfalls of beauty. How Paul reinvented himself. The important secret of acting as if.

The word "halo" is associated with saints by most people. But not by psychologists. Psychologists are well aware that what we call the halo effect has nothing to do with goodness or godliness, but with first impressions. And unfortunately, first impressions are not always good impressions.

Jackson was the new office manager. On his very first day, Lynda Mae caught his attention. She was flitting around the office, chatting with everyone and disrupting the routine. When she did settle down at her desk, she was on the telephone.

From that day on, Lynda Mae could do nothing right as far as Jackson was concerned. He saw everything she did much more negatively than he would have seen it otherwise. His first impression of her created a halo effect that radiated out to color his opinion of everything she did in the future.

If Lynda Mae had only known about the halo effect, she could have neutralized the effects of her behavior by telling Jackson that she had been asked to collect the money for the annual office picnic and that this had absorbed all her efforts that day.

The halo effect can be negative or positive. Whichever it is, it radiates out in all directions from the initial effect or impression. At its best, it helps make people think we are even better than we are.

If you are given the responsibility of rating someone on his intelligence or ability and the first time you meet that person he impresses you positively, you are likely to rate him high in other positive traits that may not be related at all to that first impression. You are likely to give him credit for being more efficient, kind, and courageous than if your first impression had been poor.

You can use the halo effect to help you succeed in business or almost anything you set your mind to—with the exception of marriage, in which the effect is mostly negative, especially in later years (see Chapter Twenty). But positive or negative, it is a key factor in the make-or-break moments of your life—in first encounters; in job interviews, business lunches, sales presentations; the first time the boss invites you home to dinner. All are crucial moments when the halo effect can determine success or failure.

It is not surprising, then, that a cardinal requisite for succeeding in business is to make a good first impression. When you are conscious of the importance of initial encounters, it is easier to learn how to take advantage of them. There are five basic rules that will help you create a positive halo for yourself during these encounters.

1. *Do your homework.* If you are meeting new people, try to find out something about them. If they are prominent in business or one of the professions or the arts, look them up in *Who's Who.* If you have access to a library with *The New York Times* on microfilm, check the index and see if the man or woman you are to meet is mentioned there. People are very much flattered when someone tells them, "I will never forget how impressed I was when I learned you were an Eagle Scout and a member of Byrd's expedition to the Pole." Or, "How is your daughter, the CPA, doing these days?" Or, "I have to tell you that I read a speech you gave before the Rotary Club in 1970—and I think it changed my life." This kind of flattery is very easy to take. And it will get you everywhere.

   Even if it is a purely social occasion, try to find out something about the people you will be meeting. And if it is a business situation, make a point of briefing yourself on the essentials of the business, how the firm is doing, what problems it faces, what successes it has enjoyed.

2. *Don't smoke.* I don't smoke myself, so perhaps I feel a little more strongly about this rule than some people. But many people today have given up cigarettes so recently that it makes them uncomfortable when others smoke in their presence. And many feel very strongly that cigarette smoke is a pollutant and they resent being exposed to it. So if you are a smoker, restrain yourself at this first meeting when the halo effect is in operation. At the very least, it is a good idea not to be the one who lights up first.

3. *Don't be late.* Many people believe that it is fashionable to arrive anywhere from twenty minutes to an hour after the appointed time for a

social engagement, but in business it is a black mark if you show up late. Not only is it discourteous, but it makes people believe that you do not value their time, and that is a sure way to create a completely negative halo effect.

4. *Get the name right, and use it more than once.* Ask if you're not sure. "Do you spell Green with an *e* on the end, or without?" "I've been looking forward to meeting you, Mr. Greene." "What do you think about the Chinese border situation, Mr. Greene?" And, in speaking to a third person, "Mr. Greene was just explaining to me why antique French furniture is a better hedge against inflation than gold."

5. *Don't talk too much, and don't interrupt.* When people are nervous, they have a tendency to chatter on and on, not letting anyone else get a word in edgewise. If you find yourself running off at the mouth, stop. That is not the way to acquire a positive halo effect. And neither is interrupting. So try not to.

It is just as important to learn how to listen as it is to discipline yourself not to talk too much. When Governor Ella Grasso of Connecticut was asked the secret of her political success, she said that one secret was "I've learned how to listen, to hear what is said—and what is left unsaid." Governor Grasso is obviously an expert at the technique known as sensitive listening. It is flattering—and effective. Instead of standing there silently while the other person talks, the sensitive listener becomes closely involved with the speaker, identifies and empathizes with him. This is how it works.

Mr. Maloney has just told you that he made his first million by the time he was twenty-nine years old. This is your cue to employ the sensitive-listening technique.

"You must have been pretty proud of yourself," the sensitive listener says. Or, even better, "I bet your parents were very proud of you."

The insensitive listener smiles and says, "Did you really? That's impressive. Truly impressive."

Now, unless Mr. Maloney has an ego as big as all outdoors (and he may very well have), there is not much for him to say to the insensitive listener's remark. It is a bit awkward for him to agree that it was a truly impressive achievement. On the other hand, he certainly does not want to pooh-pooh it and say, "Oh, it was nothing." The insensitive listener has effectively brought the conversation to a momentary halt. And while Mr. Maloney will never quite be able to put his finger on the reason, he is never going to consider that insensitive listener a prince among men.

But the sensitive listener. Well, that was something else. Either of those two remarks tells Mr. Maloney that you have heard what he said, are impressed by his achievement—and know something of how he felt when he made that million. He can now go on and agree, "Yes, I was pleased as Punch." Or, "My father was so delighted that it was all I could do to stop him from calling *The New York Times* with the big news."

Let's take another case. Mrs. Samuels tells you that she was the first woman to be appointed vice-president of her company.

"That's marvelous," the insensitive listener burbles. "The first woman vice-president, hm? Very good."

What is Mrs. Samuels to respond to that? "Yes, the first woman vice-president"? But she has just finished saying that. Or, "Yes, it was very good"? That is patting herself on the back. The insensitive listener has made it difficult for Mrs. Samuels to pursue the conversation further without ignoring that fatuous remark. She will have to consider it as nothing more than an agreeable background noise.

What would the sensitive listener say? Something like, "You must have felt great when you were promoted, but I'm sure that as the first woman in that position you faced some tricky problems."

Mrs. Samuels feels that the sensitive listener fully appreciates the triumph of being the first woman vice-president—and also appreciates that the lot of a pioneer is not easy and that breaking into this "old boy" corporate level involved more problems than not getting a key to the executive washroom.

"Why work so hard to make a good impression?" Chet asked me. Chet is head of his own electronics firm, which he started from scratch nearly twenty-five years ago, and I have known him most of my life. "It's what you know and whom you know and what you do that count. I always judge a man on the basis of his work, not on how good or bad an impression he makes or how he looks."

I did not want to contradict him bluntly, although I could have pointed out several ways in which he used the halo effect to good advantage. Chet has an engaging smile and a firm handshake. People meeting him for the first time always have the impression that he is absolutely delighted to meet them. That first impression predisposes them to like him—and want to do business with him.

His office suite is a showplace of contemporary design, with a Mies van der Rohe glass table and Corbusier chairs. His desk is a slab of highly polished black Italian marble on chrome legs. A sculpture of electronic components stands in one corner. And behind the desk hang three photographs. Chet with President Johnson. Chet with President Nixon. Chet with President Carter. Visitors can't help getting some important subliminal messages to the effect that electronics is a modern growth industry and Chet is prospering—and has very good connections. The office is designed to impress just the kind of sophisticated technologists with whom Chet does business. It creates a positive halo effect.

But I decided to bide my time, not to point out his unconscious and very effective mastery of the halo effect. A couple of weeks later I was able to show Chet that he did indeed judge people on the basis of first impressions. When I heard Roland, a young psychology instructor, mention that he planned to shave off his mop-like beard, I asked him to help me.

I called Chet and said I knew two bright young men who were interested in getting into the electronics field, perhaps as salesmen. Would he, as a favor to me, be willing to spend ten minutes with each of them?

He agreed. "If they're really bright," he said, "I might have a spot for them."

Roland showed up for his interview on time. His hair was long and shaggy, just like his beard. He wore sneakers, jeans, and a blue work shirt. He was clean but rumpled. He was courteous and spoke intelligently about his interest in the field.

The next day, Roland appeared for the second interview. He introduced himself as Hobart. If Chet were to remark about his resemblance to Roland, he was prepared to explain that Roland was his cousin. But Chet saw no resemblance between the two. "Hobart's" hair had been cut and his beard was gone. He wore a gray flannel suit with a white shirt and a striped tie. The effect was pressed and crisp.

Chet telephoned me the next day and thanked me for sending Hobart to see him. "That's the kind of young man I like to hire," he said. "But that other guy. What's his name? Roland. I was surprised you asked me to see him. He's a real hippie."

I laughed. "Hippie is out of date, Chet," I told him,

and then explained the trick I had played on him. And apologized.

"Good Lord!" he exclaimed. "You don't mean it!"

"Yes, I do," I told him. "I just had to show you that you do judge people on the basis of first impressions. Everybody does. It's the halo effect." If Chet had not been an old and dear friend, I would never have done this. But he was. And he thanked me. And made me explain the halo effect once more—in detail.

Chet was right about one thing, however, and that was "It's whom you know that counts." If your friends are prominent and prosperous, the rest of the world assumes that you are too. Or will be. And chances are that your friends will—either actively or passively—help you attain prominence and prosperity if that is what you want.

This is why admission to the Ivy League colleges is so coveted by some ambitious parents. They are aware that even if Junior is not associating with the blue-bloods and the junior plutocrats, the Ivy League aura is rubbing off on him. Or her. And it is true that later on it seldom hurts your chances of success if you can ask people to lunch at the Harvard Club or mention that you are going to the Yale–Princeton game—to root for Princeton, of course—or drop little tidbits like the fact that you dated John D. Rockefeller IV when you were at Radcliffe. None of those things ever held a person back from success. It all helps the halo.

But if you did not go to an Ivy League college, you can at least dress as if (and I'll talk more about this "as if" business later) you did. Clothes *do* make the man. And the woman. The first and most obvious impression is created by the way you dress.

Most people have had the experience of walking into a department store looking and feeling less than their best. And being ignored by the salespeople. Another time, you can walk into the same department of that department store feeling great and looking the same way. And the salespeople swarm around you.

This is the halo effect at work. It is also a very stupid reaction on the part of sales personnel. I hope that every salesperson who reads this will resolve not to be swayed by a negative halo effect. It can only hurt your sales record. The customer who looks dowdy or depressed is usually the customer who is going to spend ... his spirits or both.

... ght now. The ... n the other ... y. She may be ... ot find exactly ... ttle for some- ... ely to make a ... Mrs. Fashion-

... ment, and the ... that environ- ... elf a wardrobe ... arkable impact on the people we meet ... or socially and greatly (sometimes crucially) affects how they treat us." Harvard psychologist Zick Rubin agrees and says, "Given the power of first impressions to shape lasting opinions, it is often wise for a person who wishes to make a particular impression to present himself in that way from the outset." In other words, if you want to succeed in business, dress as if you were a success.

Mr. Molloy's research reveals that the man who wants to succeed in business should make a habit of wearing suits, not slacks and sports jackets. And that dark blue, dark gray, and pin-striped suits carry the strongest success message. He warns against wearing brown, because this tends to alienate some people.

One of his findings struck me as particularly helpful

NOT GOOD FOR STOPOVER. NOT TRANSFERABLE.

TRANSFER CAR OR BUS MUST BE BOARDED AT PROPER JUNCTION POINT.

TRANSFER MUST BE SECURED AT STATION OF ENTRY.

NOT VALID ON SURFACE VEHICLES CONNECTION WITH STATION WHERE TRANSFER ISSUED.

The use of this transfer by anyone other than the passenger for whom issued is a criminal offence.

Transfer issued on condition that in case of dispute passenger must pay fare and to young men on their way up. It has to do with raincoats. Since most young men cannot afford a coat wardrobe, their raincoat serves for all occasions. What raincoat makes the best impression? His researchers showed a scientifically selected sample of close to 1,500 people two photographs of the same man. He was wearing the same suit, tie, shirt, and shoes in both pictures. But in one photograph he had on a black raincoat; in the other, a beige raincoat. People were told that these men were twins and were asked which brother they thought was the more sucessful. Eighty percent pointed to the man wearing the beige raincoat.

So if you have only one coat and it is a raincoat, for heaven's sake get a beige one. A crisp, clean beige raincoat projects a successful, upper-middle-class image. And as Mr. Molloy says, "Clothing is a weapons system. In order to shoot the bullets, you've got to know where the target is." And the target is success.

For women, dressing for success is a somewhat more complicated matter. There are very few role models for women to pattern themselves upon. Ambitious young men can, and should, observe what the executives in their offices wear and dress accordingly. But there are not all that many women at the top, so the ambitious young woman must make her own dress rules. She should follow the masculine code in one aspect at least. And that is to dress as if (there's that "as if" again) she had already arrived at the top of her success pyramid. The woman on the way up should dress fashionably, although conservatively, and as expensively as she possibly can. She should look on her wardrobe as a blue-chip investment that will pay high dividends.

"Bankers wear suits," a young woman banker says. "And that's what I wear." A *New York Times* reporter noted, "All women on Wall Street wear three-piece suits." And a woman environmental engineer who spends a great deal of her time talking with mayors and city managers reports that she has a collection of expensive suits. "I deal chiefly with men and I want them to see me not only as an equal, but as an expert," she says. "So I work at projecting a tailored look, an expensive look. Even if it doesn't impress them, it makes me feel better about myself."

Do success-bound women have to confine themselves to tailored clothes for the rest of their working lives? Must they look like a version of the male executive? I don't think so. Women who are yearning for success will do well to take advantage of this stereotyped manner of dressing until they have established themselves. Consider it a uniform that you can discard when you make it to the top. And don't waste time and energy rebelling because you have to wear a gray flannel suit and a silk shirt when you're sitting on the dais at the annual meeting.

Just as important as the way you dress is your personal physical appearance—the way you hold yourself, the way you walk, the way you smile. One landmark study on the importance of physical appearance centered around a college dance. The students were told that a computer was matching each one of them with a blind date on the basis of shared interests. Actually, the young men and women were paired off any which way.

After the dance each student filled out a questionnaire on how he or she liked his or her date. Was it on the basis of shared interests? Not at all. According to the questionnaires, the most important factor was good looks. The students who had found their dates attractive wanted to see them again. Those who found them physically unattractive did not ever want to see them again. They did not believe that they were making this judgment on the basis of beauty alone. The students were convinced that their liking for the attractive dates was based on shared interests.

We tend to believe that attractive people have virtues

that they may not possess. We think good-looking people are more sensitive, more intelligent, more interesting, and more exciting than those who are physically mediocre. It is the halo effect again. Other studies have shown that physically attractive people are considered to have better jobs and more fun.

If a man holds himself confidently, has a warm smile, looks you straight in the eye when he speaks, and is well groomed, you will probably consider him attractive. And you undoubtedly attribute good qualities to him that he may not have.

If, however, a man is superattractive, then he may be in trouble. If you are simply terrific—tall, handsome, rich, charming, brilliant, forget about creating a positive halo effect. You have too much going for you as it is. There is a very real danger that you will make other people feel inferior, jealous and uncomfortable. They will consciously resist your charm. Your positive qualities and your good looks overload the emotional circuits.

Your job is to reassure people, show them that you are not perfect. People who have heard about how wonderful you are in advance will like you better when they meet you if you do something clumsy. Spill your drink or trip over the rug. Have a smudge (just the tiniest smudge) of ink on your cheek. Or a button off your button-down collar. If you happen to have a broken leg or arm, that will help. But don't feel you have to break a bone just to be endearing.

Women face a more complicated set of reactions. Beauty helps women get ahead—and then it trips them up if they are not careful. Men expect more of a beautiful woman. If she does not live up to their expectations, they think worse of her than of an unattractive woman who fails to live up to their expectations. That old saying "Beauty is as beauty does" has a lot of folk truth in it. Beauty will help you get there, but it won't keep you there.

Beauties tend to be less secure than the rest of us. So much is made of their looks that they are made to feel that they are valuable only as long as they are beautiful. So if you are a raving beauty and ambitious to succeed in business, work on developing confidence in your abilities. Beauty fades, but talents and competence improve with the years.

It is harder for a woman to handle this matter of being superattractive than a man. If she trips over the rug, they will whisper that she has had too much to drink. If there's a run in her panty hose, they will criticize her for being sloppy. If people think she has an unhappy private life, that may help. Sometimes talking about minor failures will neutralize the penalties of beauty, but one has to be careful here and not overdo it. The most practical thing is to play down your beauty during working hours as much as possible. And the rest of the time? Well, if you've got it, flaunt it.

With the exceptions of the superbeauties, the more attractive you are the better. Men like attractive men better than unattractive men. And they like attractive women better than unattractive women. And women feel the same way.

What do you do if you are not handsome? Join a nunnery or the Foreign Legion? No. You work on your halo effect. Make the best of what you've got and act as if you are extremely attractive.

If you are dissatisfied with your looks and the way you feel about yourself (remember, self-confidence is an important ingredient of attractiveness), then I suggest that you reinvent yourself. And I mean that quite literally.

Paul reinvented himself. He was twenty-seven and shy, still plagued by "adolescent" acne. He had a dull job in a discount record store and a pitiful salary. And no girlfriend. Paul was not actively ugly. That could have been a plus. He was nondescript.

Yet behind that anonymous facade blazed fierce ambition. Paul wanted to succeed in business. He daydreamed about sitting at the head of a long conference table, leading his associates to profitable decisions. If anyone had known of Paul's secret ambition, he or she would have laughed.

But today Paul sits at that conference table he used to daydream about. Not at the head. Not yet. But he is sure he will make it to the head of the table one of these years or even months.

What happened? He read a magazine article about a psychologist who counseled his patients to "act as if." If they wanted to be popular, they should act as if they were popular. If they wanted to be successful lawyers, they should act as if they were successful lawyers. The "act as if" technique is simply a way of creating a positive halo effect. Paul read and reread the article. It made a lot of sense to him. And he decided to follow the advice.

He knew all his drawbacks and deficits. But he had never done anything to remedy them. Now he made an appointment to see a dermatologist about his acne. He went to an expensive barbershop and had his hair not just cut but styled. He bought two new suits.

When he showed up at the record store the following Monday, his boss looked twice. Paul seemed to be another man. The dermatologist had given him a program of skin care and prescriptions for ointments. In just two days, his skin looked clearer. He was wearing a dark blue pin-striped suit. He looked more like a prosperous young lawyer or stockbroker than someone who sold discount rock albums.

"What happened?" the boss asked. "Did your rich uncle die?"

"No," Paul said. "I don't have a rich uncle. And I have to make more money." He explained that he was going to start job hunting.

The change started right then and there. The boss said he would give Paul a raise. Paul said it was not just the money, he wanted a chance to get ahead. After some discussion, the boss suggested that Paul might like to buy into the business.

Paul went over the books with an accountant, consulted a lawyer, talked with a couple of banks, and decided that it was a good opportunity.

The whole thing was like a magic shot of confidence, all that Paul needed to start his climb to success. In a couple of years, the store was bought by a chain. Paul was part of the deal. In another few years, the chain was merged into one of the big recording companies. And again Paul was part of the deal.

No one would recognize Paul today at thirty-nine as the Paul of twelve years ago. He truly has reinvented himself. And the first step in the making of the new Paul was using the halo effect constructively. By acting as if, he was able to reach his goal.

The halo effect is one of the most powerful psychological tools at your disposal. And like all power tools, it must be handled carefully, because it has a destructive as well as a constructive potential.

So check your halo effect.

Do you look like the kind of person you would like to know? Would like to do business with? Would like to have on your side in a negotiation?

Do you dress so that people could mistake you for the boss—not for the office boy or receptionist?

Can you recognize the make-or-break encounters early enough so that you can do the necessary homework to create a positive halo effect?

Do you act as if you were the success you want to be?

If the answer to any of these questions is no, then you had better get busy and adjust your halo.

CHAPTER EIGHT

The Seduction of Total Commitment

The quality that opens the door to the executive suite and may close the door on marriage. How one man uses the law of averages to help him succeed. The total-commitment high called flow that helps you work more effectively and creatively. How to condition yourself to switch into the flow state. Why successful people are healthier. The difference between hard work and total commitment. How to capitalize on inertia to get to the top.

Are you willing to work hard in order to succeed? To go all out? To sacrifice certain pleasures because your time and energy must be devoted to your goal? Will you be happy to make these sacrifices?

If the answer is yes, you want to go all out, then you are right on target. You have found the right goal for the inner you. If, however, you think you will begrudge giving up evenings to work and resent having to pass up weekend fun, then think again. You may not want to climb to the top of the ladder, just part way. Your true goal probably lies elsewhere.

People who succeed in business have the single-minded devotion to their goal that is best described as total commitment. Some people refer to these over-achievers as workaholics. But that implies illness, and if you are doing what you want to do more than anything else in the world, why should you punish yourself by cutting down on the things that make you happy?

Success in business does not necessarily preclude a happy marriage, but those men and women who want to go to the very top, who play for the highest stakes, often find that their total commitment leaves no room for marriage. On the other hand, those men (not women) who want what I call "corporate success" rather than "entrepreneurial success" should know that they will probably advance faster if they are married than if they are not.

Psychologists retained by large corporations to test men and women being considered for promotion to executive ranks look for one quality more than any other. If the candidate has it, that clinches the promotion. If he doesn't, then he's out of the running. This pivotal quality is total commitment, the ability and desire to work to top capacity. They want people who scoff at 40-hour weeks, who work 60-, 80-, and 100-hour weeks because they find their work exciting and rewarding and they are seeking success. Total commitment is the common denominator among successful men and women. Its importance cannot be overestimated.

Take Joe, for instance. Joe is an insurance salesman. He has been called "the greatest insurance salesman in the business."

His secret?

"I put every ounce of energy into my work," he says. "Right from the start, I worked ten to twelve hours a day, seven days a week. There just wasn't anything else that mattered. Everything that I do is associated with selling life insurance.

"When I started out," Joe says, "I was told that if I called seventy-five people, I could expect to get twenty-five appointments. And that ten of those twenty-five appointments would probably fall through, leaving me about fifteen. And I should be able to see three of those fifteen. And that would be a good week's work, they told me.

"I changed the numbers," he says. "I call seventy-five people a day, not a week. I spend five and six hours on the phone. And I spend another five or six seeing people. The law of averages works. The more calls I make, the more sales I make."

Successful men and women must have good health and boundless energy. Climbing to the top demands strength, whether it's to the top of Mount Everest or to the top of the XYZ Corporation. People are born with differing energy reserves. And the man or woman who tires fast, burns out easily would do well to reset his or her goals. Or limit them. Instead of aiming to be chairman of an international multiconglomerate, settle for being president of a small bakery chain or even owner of a neighborhood bakery. For the lower-energy individual, succeeding in business could very well take the form of making it to department chief instead of president. These lesser goals are honorable and satisfying. The men and women who are content with a smaller degree of business success will have richer lives. They are the ones who have time to read and go to the theater, to go hiking with their children, to build strong family ties, to indulge in the joys of friendship, to nurture human values. But the others, those with boundless energy and ambition who want to soar to the top, do not see their total commitment as a sacrifice. To their way of thinking, they are gaining. They feel fulfilled and happy.

Sarah Caldwell, the famed director of the Opera Company of Boston, is one of these. "I love what I do," she says. "I can work for days without sleep because I get so caught up with every detail of producing and conducting an opera. Once in a while, when everything is just right, there's a moment of magic. People can live on moments of magic."

She was referring to moments of magic on the stage, when everything comes together. Her business happens to be opera, and she is one of the handful of people who have made it to the pinnacle—and the only woman. But in every business there are moments of magic that people with total commitment experience, moments of magic that are the result of what psychologists refer to as flow. And flow is such a peak experience that it is a very strong argument for not resisting the seduction of total commitment.

To most of the world, total commitment is a sign of misplaced values or even disease, and its practitioners are workaholics, but as I said at the beginning of this chapter, these men and women are doing exactly what they want to do and loving every minute of it. They are a breed apart. They are strivers. They are always reaching—higher than the next person, higher than the last time. And while their marriages may not be spectacularly sucessful, they find the rewards of their drive staggering. Money. Influence. Power. Prestige. And the joys of flow.

Just what is flow? And what are these joys? Sarah Caldwell described it very well as "moments of magic." It is analogous to the high that joggers experience. A researcher has defined flow as "a sensation present when we act with total involvement." During flow, action follows on action according to an internal logic that seems to need no conscious intervention on the part of the participant. There is no hurry; there are no distracting demands on attention. Moment flows into moment. Past and future disappear. So does the distinction between oneself and the activity.

There was a report in one of the psychological journals several years ago about a surgeon who was so deeply involved in the surgery he was performing that he was completely unaware that part of the operating-room ceiling collapsed. It was only after the last stitch was taken in the last incision that he took a deep breath, stretched, look around—and asked in surprise, "What's all that plaster on the floor?" He had been in a state of flow.

One of the pioneering studies on flow came about because a researcher wanted to know why some people play so hard. What do activities as different as chess and backgammon, tennis and handball, volleyball and football have in common that makes people give their all without any thought of reward? Plato asked this question centuries ago—and never came up with a satisfactory answer. Freud asked the same question—and never came up with an answer either. But Dr. Mihaly Czikazentmihalyi of the University of Chicago isolated the common denominator. He questioned 175 people— 30 rock climbers, 30 basketball players, 30 modern dancers, 30 male chess players, 25 female chess players, 30 composers of modern music. What was it, he asked, that they enjoyed so much about composing music or playing chess or climbing steep rock faces? Was it the prestige? The glamour? The prospect of winning? It turned out that the chief attraction was the altered state of being they enjoyed while deeply involved in chess or basketball or whatever.

When people achieve the state that we call flow, they are relaxed, but at the same time feel energetic and fresh. Their ability to concentrate increases markedly. They feel very much in control of themselves and their world. Like happiness, flow is a by-product. The first requirement is to work as hard as you can at something that presents a challenge. Not an overwhelming challenge, but the kind that stretches you just a little, makes you realize that you are doing something better today than you did it yesterday or the last time you tried to do it. Another prerequisite is a significant span of uninterrupted time. It is virtually impossible to switch into a flow state in less than half an hour. And it is absolutely impossible if you are bedeviled by interruptions.

It is possible, with practice, to switch yourself into flow by using a conditioning device in much the same way that you condition yourself to learn effectively. The secret is to analyze previous occasions when you enjoyed those magic moments. Was there any common denominator? Once you have isolated the common denominator, you can set the stage for flow.

Margaret learned how to do this. She was a lobbyist based in Washington, D.C., working for a Western conservation group. One night she leaned back in her chair and stretched. It felt good. She had been working hard, pulling together a report on a bill before Congress that would set up new standards for the disposal of wastes from paper mills—a bill that, if passed, would have a direct and adverse effect on the lumber and pulp companies.

She had outlined the present status of the bill, the lobbying efforts of the lumber and pulp interests, and her own activities and had suggested certain steps to bring the situation to the attention of the public, whose sure-to-be-indignant response might sway the legislators into placing conservation above corporate profits.

Now she glanced at the clock. And then took a closer look. Four o'clock! In the morning! She checked her watch. The clock was right. She had been working on the report ever since she had finished supper the previous evening—and she could have sworn that she had been at her desk for no more than two or three hours.

She had been so engrossed in what she was doing that the time had raced by.

Margaret had experienced this before. There had been days at the office now and again when she had looked up to find it empty and to realize that it was way after quitting time. On those days, she had always been so much caught up in whatever she was doing that the lunch hour slipped by without her even being conscious that she was hungry.

By analyzing these episodes, she realized that they were similar, each triggered by the near-completion of a project or a phase of a project when she had gathered all the necessary data and was ready to start summing up the problem, outlining the positions taken by opposing interests and making her recommendations for action. She also realized that it happened on days that were relatively quiet in the office—no crises, no important meetings, no out-of-town VIPs.

Once she had this clear in her mind, Margaret made a point of arranging her work so that she could take advantage of flow more frequently. Whenever she reached the trigger stage, she took her work home so that she could count on a stretch of uninterrupted time. And when she sat down at her desk on those days, she also used a verbal conditioning device, saying, "Now I am going to concentrate as hard as I can." It did not always work. There were times when she labored through her reports. But more and more often, she was able to glide into flow, where her concentration increased significantly.

No one can—or should—remain in a constant state of flow. It would be too draining. Like an orgasm prolonged past endurance. The sexual analogy is not a frivolous one, for flow is not confined to work. The potential is inherent in everything we do that demands concentration—playing games, painting, writing, learning, and, of course, sex. It is a truly euphoric state, the ecstasy peak of total commitment.

It is also a stressful state, because the whole organism is at a high pitch, but this is healthy stress. Researchers have found that successful people are healthier than those who are unsuccessful or only middlingly so. One study of very successful men showed that their mortality rate was one third less than that of men in comparable age groups who had not achieved great success. And stress, so often considered to be debilitating, is a positive factor in their health. Some stress, of course, is debilitating, but it is important to realize that it can be healthful as well. Successful people enjoy the stress of coping with difficulties. They are attracted to what one researcher refers to as "the call of controlled risk." They seek it because they are full of energy. They feel more vital when they are active. The active person's brain functions better than the sedentary person's brain, just as the active body functions better than the sedentary body. So flow stress makes for health. Just as physical exertion does. Just as change does. And, just as all of these stress factors are dangerous in excess, so is flow. But don't worry about it. Your system is self-protective. You will not be able to switch yourself into a flow state often enough to cause undue, unhealthy stress.

"It is all very well to talk about total commitment and the euphoria of flow," a businessman objected, "but I know men and women who work like donkeys and never get anywhere."

"So do I," I agreed with him. "And it's because they work like donkeys. Hard work is not enough. You have to have a goal. And you have to know how to make your hard work pay off."

Total commitment is not just hard work: it is total involvement. Building a rock wall is backbreaking work. There are some people who build rock walls all their lives. And when they die, there are miles of walls, mute testimonials to how hard these people worked. But there are other men who build rock walls and all the time that they are placing one rock on top of another they have a vision in their minds, a goal. It may be a terrace with roses climbing over the rock walls and chairs set out for lazy summer days. Or the rock wall may enclose an apple orchard or mark a boundary. When they have finished, they have more than a wall. It is the goal that makes the difference, as Beth's and Trudy's experiences show.

Both got jobs as stewardesses. Both wanted to see the world. But Trudy wanted something more. She wanted to go into business. She thought she might like to have her own travel agency or perhaps work for a hotel chain—something that involved travel. She was not sure exactly what. This job was her first step toward her goal. She would be traveling and learning about the world's great cities and about the kinds of people who traveled—where they liked to go and why. She had a marvelous time and soaked up knowledge like the proverbial sponge. When passengers asked her questions about where they were going, she had all kinds of advice. "I was just there two weeks ago," she would say, recommending a restaurant, "and the food was really terribly good. I must have gained five pounds." She kept a notebook of her favorite places and loved to tell people about special shops and off-the-tourist-track restaurants.

An airline executive who was flying incognito to check out service and personnel watched Trudy at work. She was quick and competent, always helpful. When she was not serving meals, Trudy would be holding a baby so its mother could stretch her legs or answering passengers' questions about their destination.

"That girl's too good to waste as a stewardess," the inspector said when he returned from the trip. "She's a walking encyclopedia of what to do and see in every city we fly to. And she works her head off." A few weeks later, Trudy was offered a promotion. Her new job was working on a series of city-by-city travel pamphlets. Today, ten years later, she is head of her own travel agency, one of the most successful small agencies in the business.

And what about Beth? Beth loved her job. Becoming a stewardess had been her goal. But in time she became disenchanted. It was just plain hard work—rushing up and down the aisles serving meals and taking trays away, answering questions, coping with drunks and bores and airsick passengers. Ten years later, Beth is still a stewardess. A very hardworking, conscientious one. She now has another goal: marriage. She figures that is the only way out of her dead-end job.

In most respects, Beth worked just as hard as Trudy did. But Beth had no goal. And people who do not know where they want to go usually end up going nowhere.

If you know what it is you want out of life and you are totally committed to working for it, then all sorts of opportunities open up. Many of them open up because of inertia. Other people's inertia, not yours. Everyone is basically lazy. Even the men and women who are blessed with boundless energy and burning to be successful. The secret is to understand this and promise yourself that you will not give in to your laziness—and will make it easy for the other fellow to give in to his. The way to do this is to maximize the possibility of success for the other person—minimize the amount of effort he or she will have to make to achieve that success.

Erich worked for a large accounting firm, which had a reputation for getting every last penny's worth out of its employees. "We're being asked to do too much," Erich's colleagues would complain. "This business of working late every night is crazy. They should hire more people."

Erich listened and worked just a little harder. He decided that the only way to stand out from the other accountants was to do more work and to do it better. Searching for ways to do it better, he came up with a plan for reorganizing the work flow that would result in increased productivity. He worked out a table of reorganization, put it in memo form, and gave it to his boss.

He had thought it out very carefully. His memo was neatly typed, but personal. Erich had done the typing himself, not asked one of the girls from the typing pool. He wanted it to be clear that this memo was for his boss alone, that the boss did not have to worry that Erich would go over his head and show it to someone higher up.

More than that, Erich had not just outlined his plan for reorganization, he had indicated just how to achieve the reorganization. If the boss liked the plan, all he would have to do would be say okay. Erich would take care of the rest. The boss liked the plan. He and Erich talked about it over sandwiches one night when they were working late. Erich indicated that if the office were reorganized, the increased productivity would make the boss look good to his superiors. He made it easy for the boss to say yes. Erich had done all the work. He had taken advantage of the boss's inertia. Erich's plan worked so well that the boss got a promotion. And who got promoted right along with him? Erich, of course. The boss needed someone who would make him look good. Erich is now on the executive level where he can talk to the other executives as an equal. And he got there several years ahead of the normal promotion schedule because he took advantage of the power of inertia.

This is very important for the man or woman on the way up. The person who succeeds fastest is the one who does the "too much" and gets credit for it where it counts.

The moral of this chapter is—don't think of total commitment as a disease; think of it as the only way of life that will result in your attaining your goal of being fabulously successful in business. You will find that the sacrifices are insignificant in view of the fact that you are doing just what you want to do most. So when it comes to the seduction of total commitment, yield.

CHAPTER NINE

And Then There Is Discrimination

How to use women's special strengths for business success. The instinctive male fear of female competence. How to use the divide-and-conquer technique to survive in a masculine world. What women can learn from men about flattery. How to establish a businesswoman's equivalent of the "old boy network." Why a woman executive should not lunch with the secretaries. How to escape from the female ghetto. What a sponsor can do for you—and for herself or himself. The importance of learning the rules of the game. Four key rules for women who want to win.

No matter how successful a woman is, men are more successful. Men earn a shocking 75 percent more than women. Even men who never went beyond the eighth grade earn more than women who have completed four years of college. And the executive level of big business is a virtual male monopoly. There are exceptions, of course, but heartbreakingly few of them. And of those exceptions, a significant proportion have to be recognized as tokens—"We've got nothing against women. Why, we've even got a girl [sometimes referred to as "gal"] on our board of directors."

The fact is that there is discrimination against women in the business world. There is no point in laboring this.

It is a fact, pure and simple. It is harder for women to get to the top, and it takes longer. And it is harder for both male and female members of minority groups to get to the top. The examples and techniques in this chapter are as applicable for members of minority groups as they are for women. I concentrate on women's problems, however, because of the sheer weight of numbers. They represent a good half of the population, a half that does not enjoy the blessings of equal rights and equal opportunities as yet.

There is no point in carrying a chip on your shoulder because of discrimination. It won't help. What will help is to be aware of the problems you face and learn how to handle them. The techniques I have outlined in previous chapters are equally appropriate for men and women. There is no sex difference in motivation or learning or in the kinds of manipulation involved in using these techniques. These psychological tools can help you combat and minimize the discrimination you face in the business world.

Women have not learned to capitalize on their own special strengths. We are tremendously strong and capable. Unfortunately, the things women are most successful at are things that society does not value highly. But these abilities are transferable. They can be transferred to areas where they will be valued highly. Women must be aware of this.

Take friendship, for instance. Women have great talent for friendship. They have always been close to each other, shared chores, exchanged knowledge. Even in the animal kingdom, the females help one another. Males don't. In most marriages the wife is the bridge to the rest of the world. If she does not make friends, the couple have few if any friends. Men tend to confine their friends—more correctly described as acquaintances—to those men who can be useful to them in business. But women have friends of many kinds. And they are loyal to them. This ability to make and keep friends is of tremendous use in the business world. Executive women can use their talent for friendship to increase cooperation and get the job done better and faster. As one female psychoanalyst tells women, "Use your abilities to support each other as you move into greater activity and scope and face new kinds of power struggles and rivalries."

And then there is managerial ability. A study of the talents required to bring up children and manage a household—mechanical, organizational, and creative—revealed that homemaking requires such a vast range of capabilities that if a man utilized them in business, he would be considered a fantastic success. And if a woman utilizes these abilities in business, she can *be* a fantastic success.

Women know a lot more about what people are interested in than men do. Men are not as tuned in to the interests of others as women are. Too often, the end consumer is less important to men than office politics and infighting over budgets and office space. They forget that their job is to focus on how to get the customer to buy the firm's product instead of the rival's product. Women do not lose sight of the end goal. And they can identify with the consumer, whether he or she is in the market for detergents or baling wire, deodorants or soybeans, disposable diapers or insurance policies.

With all these strengths, what is holding women back? Plenty.

There has been so much written about the need for female assertiveness in magazine articles and other books that I do not feel it necessary to go over that familiar ground here. Sociologist Pauline Bart summed it up neatly. "The way you have to behave in the business or professional world," she says, "emphasizes qualities that women have not been trained to emphasize." And a dozen or so studies showing that the women who succeed in business are usually firstborn or only children who were close to their fathers, who were considered tomboys, who absorbed the rough-and-tumble, highly competitive team spirit characteristics of the male life-style bear her out. Even the women who slip easily into the masculine work-style have more than their share of problems. It is a case of damned if you do and damned if you don't. "It's all right until you get the job and become an instant man," says Bart. "I remember one teacher at Berkeley who constantly got awards. All the men in the department made fun of her behind her back and called her 'brass ovaries.' "

Women who are described or accused in similar terms should consider the origin of this hostility. Sheer male fear. As Dr. Jean Baker Miller, author of *Toward a New Psychology of Women*, explains, "When women move out of their restricted place, they threaten men in a very profound sense with the need to reintegrate many of the essentials of human development—the essentials that women have been carrying for the total society. Those things have been warded off and now become doubly fearful because they look as if they will entrap men in emotions, weakness, sexuality, vulnerability, the need for care. At a more obvious level, women's self-directed effectiveness will lead to the obvious need to re-examine many supports, including cheap labor, that women have provided so readily."

There is no need to recite the dreary litany of injustices that ambitious women must overcome. They have been written about and experienced often enough so that no woman—and no man either—can be unaware of the situation. What I want to talk about are the psychological techniques that women can use to change this uneven balance of power.

One psychiatrist studied the interactions in offices where one woman worked with a group of men of equal rank and responsibility. In every case the men resisted the woman's attempt to be part of the group. If the woman showed anger or hurt, they shrugged it off by saying she was either a Women's Libber or a neurotic bitch—or both.

The most effective technique for coping with this problem of being the lone—and ostracized—woman in a formerly all-male stronghold is probably the age-old one of Divide and Conquer.

Candace used this successfully. She was the first woman stockbroker in a very dignified New Orleans firm. The other brokers would have nothing to do with her. Research memos somehow got "lost" before they reached her desk. Her colleagues "forgot" to tell her about staff meetings. This went on for two months. Then Candace decided to do something about it.

She acted carefully. One of her colleagues, somewhat older than the others, had consistently treated her with more courtesy. She knew that it was simply a reflex, but she also knew that his inbred courtesy would make it difficult for him to refuse a direct request for a favor.

She asked him to lunch with her. "I have a client who wants to invest in machine-tool companies. I know you specialize in that area. Would you let me take you out to lunch and ask you a few questions?"

How could he say no? Candace had no such client. She had tailored her request to the other broker's specialty. They lunched. Candace asked questions. He answered. She listened. She employed the sensitive-listening technique, never letting the conversation drift into a dead end, always helping him to talk more about himself and his interests. At the end of a pleasant two hours, she thanked him for his time and his help. She complimented him on his grasp of the field. And he glowed.

Several days later she told him she had investigated a couple of the situations he had mentioned and found that they were just right for her fictional client. And then she offered him a reward, a quid pro quo. She told him of a small company whose development she had been following. It was about to make important news. He was appreciative. And so, as it developed, were several of his clients whom he advised to invest in the company.

Candace then proceeded to ask two more of her aloof male colleagues to lunch under similar circumstances, asking them for advice in a field where they had some expertise. And, always, flattering them and giving them a good tip a few days later.

Today she is accepted by her colleagues—and she should be. She does more business than any one of them. The Divide and Conquer technique works beautifully if you use it skillfully. Candace did.

And just a word about flattery, another tool that Candace used to good effect. It will get you everywhere. There has been a lot written about yes-men to the effect that their bosses see through them and scorn them. This is not true. There have been several studies on apple polishers or brown-nosers, following their careers for as long as five and ten years. Despite an executive's professed dislike for flattery—"I don't want people around me who yes me. I want people who have ideas and are creative"—guess who is still working for that executive five and ten years later when he is at the top of the corporate ladder? The apple polisher. Every time his boss makes a move up, the apple polisher is brought along.

Women have a lot to learn from men about flattery. A typical man's compliment goes like this: Randolph tells Pamela, "You look super tonight."

A typical woman's compliment goes like this: Serena also thinks that Pamela looks super. But what does she say? "Oh, what a beautiful dress!" she exclaims.

Randolph wins the flattery contest hands down. He directed his compliment toward Pamela. Serena directed hers toward Pamela's dress. It is the person, not the object, who should be flattered.

"But I can't tell the boss he looks great," one woman objected. "Yes, you can," I told her. "And he'll love it." However, since men prefer achievement compliments to appearance compliments, the best way to stroke your boss is to say something like "I read your report last night. It's the best analysis of the problem I've seen." For more flattery techniques, see Chapter Sixteen.

The opposite side of the coin of Divide and Conquer is equally helpful to women. It is Strength in Numbers. A young woman banker realized that there was absolutely no way she could break into the "old boy network"—the lunches, the clubs and the executive washroom where the men gathered to gossip and share information. So she decided to establish her own network.

She asked three women bankers to her apartment for drinks one evening and broached the idea of forming a Women's Bankers Association. They liked the idea and decided to have another meeting to which each of the original four would ask another woman in banking. From that nucleus of eight grew an active group of more than twenty women in banking. Not all of them had achieved executive level. Some were tellers, others loan officers, a couple were vice-presidents. They represented seven banking establishments in the city, and each woman was able to extend her acquaintanceship horizontally and vertically beyond the limits of her own bank. The association meets for dinner one night a month in a private dining room of a downtown restaurant. The members talk about their jobs, their problems, positions that are opening up, and exchange other mutually helpful information. They have established a network of women of like interests and like goals—what one writer has described as a "new girl network."

Similar groups have been formed and are being formed in other businesses and professions. In New

York, for instance, there are the Women's Media Group, which includes women from the worlds of publishing, journalism, television, and radio, and The Financial Women's Association. There is the Organization of Women Executives in Los Angeles. These groups are relatively easy to organize. There is very little red tape or expense involved, and they can yield tremendous benefits.

One of the most important benefits is dispelling the isolation most women experience when they reach executive rank. As one woman banker says, "Women from middle management on up tend to be very alienated. They have had to adjust themselves to a situation in which they are clearly not one of the boys. But they cannot return to being one of the girls." And that is very true. If you want to make your way up the management ladder, you cannot associate with the receptionists and secretaries. You must associate with your peers or superiors. And that can be difficult, sometimes close to impossible, for a woman. If her peers are all men, the upbound woman must expect to lunch alone until she has established herself as equal and accepted in the office unless she has a network of peers on the outside, such as the women bankers, the media group, and the women executives have established for themselves.

It is even difficult for those highly qualified women with a Master of Business Administration degree to earn acceptance as equals in most companies. And even harder to gain equal consideration when promotions are made. One oil-company executive with this coveted degree reports, "In our company management does not recognize women as having management potential. And they don't put them on the high-potential lists, which would enable them to move up fast. No matter how highly qualified you are," she says, "it is really whom you know or whom your boss knows that can help you gain promotion."

This is absolutely true. And the most effective way of lifting yourself out of the female ghetto is to find yourself a sponsor. Ambitious men have always done this. They ally themselves with a rising corporate star, and as his fortunes wax, so do theirs. Again this is more difficult for a woman, because there are not enough women in top jobs to act as sponsors, which means that women must look for male sponsorship. And, just for the record, sponsorship without any sexual connotation. Sex is not the road to success in business.

What is a sponsor? This a gray area, certainly not one to be found in the personnel charts. But when you have someone important behind you, says one senior vice-president who had a very influential sponsor in his early days, "a variety of people become impressed with you. You see the effect of the support at several levels. You get offered special jobs by powerful people. You are pulled aside and don't have to go through channels."

And how do you get one? Sometimes a top executive is looking for a woman with impressive credentials whom he can use to show that the firm does not discriminate against women. There is no reason you should not take advantage of his need. Just promise yourself that you will not be a token, but a fully functioning individual. Other male executives sponsor women because they think a woman will be more faithful to their interests than a man.

But a woman does not have to sit around hoping and waiting for a sponsor to pick her from the wallflower ranks. And she should not. Passivity will get you nowhere. The ambitious woman will take the initiative and use her psychological tools to procure herself a sponsor.

Business is basically a game played for very high stakes. To succeed, a woman must learn the rules of the game and play it for all she's worth—employing every psychological tool at her disposal. I advise women not only to learn the rules of the game, but also to make use of my four Women's Rules for Success in the world of business, which is still a man's world.

1. Work hard. And make sure that management is aware of your total commitment. This involves working late and expanding your horizons beyond your present job. Learn everything you can about the business. Don't settle for reading the annual report. Analyze that report. What does it mean to the corporation? To the stockholders? To you? Be aware of sales figures and earnings. Get acquainted with as many people as you can in the business—in and out of your own firm.

2. Set your goals. Make a game plan. Where do you want to be next year? And the year after? What do you want to be earning three years from now? Ask your male colleagues about their goals. Most of them will enjoy talking about their long-term career plans. Analyze their goals and then rethink yours. Perhaps you were not ambitious enough.

3. Make sure that you are noticed—favorably. Dress for success. Learn how to speak up for your point of view. And if you don't have anything to say, learn to ask questions in order to attract attention.

4. Don't try to be one of the boys. Be yourself. Capitalize on your female strengths and use the psychological tools you have acquired to deal with male chauvinism as well as to climb the ladder to success.

STOP: Do Not Turn This Page

Please do not turn this page unless you have taken the Success Potential Test referred to on page 37. The following chapter tells you how to increase your potential for success. And how to acquire success potential if you lack it. So if you have not yet taken the test please skip pages 93 through 101 and turn directly to Chapter Eleven, which starts on page 103.

After you have completed the Success Potential Test, you can turn back to Chapter Ten. In the meantime, please don't cheat yourself. You will get what you want out of this book only if you use it properly.

If you *have* taken the SPT, however, do turn the page and learn how to make the most of your success potential.

tered, but I almost fainted. I'd never done anything like it before. And I knew that if I didn't do a good job, I'd never be asked to do anything like it again—or given any important projects. But I didn't know where to start. For a couple of days I was panicked. Then I decided: Okay, it's like everything else. You take it a step at a time."

That thought permitted Nancy to energize herself. She called a travel agent; described the kind of place she was looking for, the price range, the dates involved, the size conference room and the service that would be necessary.

"The travel agent was very helpful," she said. "He came up with five or six suggestions. I eliminated four because transportation would be too complicated. Of the remaining two, Resort A had more facilities than Resort B, and since all the other factors were equal, I settled on Resort A.

"After that it was easy to go on. I sent a memo to the boss describing the resort and outlining the facilities. He returned it saying, 'Great!' and I was off and running."

Once Nancy had her first taste of accomplishment feedback, she was ready for more. She discovered that as she buttoned up each phase and detail of the sales meeting, she got the same accomplishment feedback. Each step-by-step achievement fed into the next.

The secret here was that Nancy had broken down her assignment into step-by-step goals. Each goal that she reached represented a small success and gave her the desired accomplishment feedback.

Now suppose you are one of the many people who took the ring-toss test and discovered that they had no success potential. You are shocked. Even shattered. You never thought of yourself that way before. Here you have set yourself a goal, something that you really want—to succeed in business—and you learn that you have little or no success potential. What do you do now?

First of all, you do not give up your goal. Not now. Think about your goal. How did you settle on it? Did you just say, "Oh, I know what I want more than anything else. I want to succeed in business"? Or did you arrive at your goal through the diagnostic route of the Quick List Technique?

If it was a spontaneous decision, I suggest trying the Quick List Technique. You may discover aspects of yourself that you were not aware of previously. It may not be business success that you really want. You may want to run a cheese shop, do research, write a novel, teach—one of any number of things. And if so, you refocus your energies. But if your Quick Lists show that you really do want to succeed in business, then you can increase your motivation and your success potential. You can change yourself so that you can get what you want.

And how do you do that? In the same way that Nancy set up her firm's annual sales conference. By giving yourself a taste of success. By enjoying accomplishment feedback. The more success you have, the more you will want. It is not hard to arrange for accomplishment feedback. Tell yourself that you care, that you really want to succeed, that you want to go all out for success. *Then make sure that you succeed at the very next challenge that comes your way.*

And to make sure that you succeed, I suggest that you provide the challenge for yourself. Set the stage for success. Here are some things you can do.

Tell yourself that you are going to clean off your desk and get caught up with everything before you go home Friday night. And then do it. Even if you have to sit there until eleven. And enjoy the good feeling of accomplishment.

Promise yourself that you are going to make an extra sales call every day this week. And then do it. You will feel good for having made the extra calls, and they will probably result in extra sales—a double accomplishment feedback.

Arrange to lunch with someone who can brief you on aspects of your firm or business that you are not familiar with. You will learn something. You will have called yourself to the attention of someone who may be able to help you at some future juncture. And you have an opportunity to create a successful halo effect.

Once you start thinking this way, you will be able to come up with dozens of ways to build success into your life. Program your life so that you will have at least one success a week. This will give you not only a taste, but a positive hunger for success. And then? Then just set yourself more and more ambitious goals until you reach that goal you were aiming at all the time. The top of the ladder.

It can be done. There is one success story that I find especially inspiring because it shows how one can really do what one wants and that it is never too late. When a man or woman finally decides to make the break and do what he really wants most in life, life can change and become much more worth living—emotionally, physically, and financially.

Avery seemed to have absolutely no potential for success. He grew up during the Depression. He had just started working when World War II broke out and he was drafted. After the war, jobs were hard to find. There were thousands, hundreds of thousands of other young veterans looking for jobs. The best opening Avery could find was in the mail room of a printing firm. Eventually he was promoted to an opening in the billing department. And there he stayed year after year. He was bored. And yet he did not dare leave. Where else would he go? What could he do? At forty-five? With a family to support?

Then he heard that a local real estate agent needed someone to answer the telephone weekends. He found the atmosphere stimulating. The business of acquiring listings and selling houses was fascinating to him. And the realtor discovered that Avery was a real asset. He had a knack of suggesting houses that appealed to clients. After a few months, he brought in a couple of listings. At that point the realtor asked Avery, "How would you like to join the firm on a full-time basis?"

There was nothing Avery would have liked better. Real estate was like a marvelous game, matching properties to clients and making deals. But a real estate agent had to take a course and pass an exam and he had neither the time nor the money. "Why not?" the boss asked. "I think you'll make a crackerjack salesman. Why not take a chance on yourself?"

And Avery did. He took the course at night, passed the exam, and quit his job at the printing firm. Avery was a great salesman. Every success generated a new success. After a couple of years, he switched to commercial real estate and traveled around a four-state area looking for factory sites, supermarket sites, possible locations for motels and restaurants. Twelve years later Avery is making more than $100,000 a year. But that is not the only change. He is nearly sixty, but he looks younger than he did at forty-five. He exudes confidence and enthusiasm. He is happier, healthier, and much, much wealthier.

I listened to him addressing a college graduating class recently. He told them the story of how he had started his new career at forty-five. With no experience. And with very little confidence in himself.

"I'm going to tell you the secret of my success," he told the young graduates. "And I want you to use it.

"Every morning when I shave," Avery said, "I look

at myself in the mirror and I say over and over, 'You must succeed. You're going to succeed.' I've said that every morning for the last twelve years. And it works. I have succeeded."

Avery had instinctively found the most effective psychological tool for increasing his initially very low success potential. He thought himself into success.

You can too.

CHAPTER ELEVEN

Twenty-five Rules for Succeeding in Business

The profile of success. What to do if you do not conform to the success profile. The first eleven rules for success. The single most valuable tool for success. How to improve your communication field. The hunches that must be obeyed. The plight of Polly, the pool typist. Why you should treat yourself to success symbols before you have earned them. How to learn to make effective decisions. The importance of high visibility. Why you should not marry the boss's daughter. Why you should not marry the boss's son.

If you are the oldest child, or better still, an only child; if you had a difficult childhood; if your father was ambitious and relatively successful; if you went to Harvard and got average marks; if you suffer from gout, you grit your teeth, and the magic went out of your marriage years ago—you are probably very successful. And generally healthy. And happy. Despite that ho-hum marriage. Despite the long hours you work. Because you are a success, and that is what you want more than anything else. This is no arbitrary profile of success, but one based upon the findings of literally hundreds of studies. If this cluster of circumstances fits your life, the odds are all on your side if what you want is to succeed in business.

103

Study after study has shown that only or oldest children form a significant majority of the population of success and that there is something about a difficult or unhappy childhood that is positively beneficial if you want to make it to the top. Researchers at The Human Development Institute in Berkeley, California, followed 413 men and women for nearly two decades. The most successful people in the group, they discovered, were the ones who had been unhappy or experienced significant difficulties as children.

Yale men may scoff and Princeton graduates may expostulate, but the cream of the executive crop went to Harvard. Seven percent of the 74,000 top executives in the United States are Harvard men. Seven percent does not sound like a lot, but just take a look at the top ten universities and the number of executives they produced (the figures are based on a survey by Standard & Poor's).

Harvard	5,017
New York University	2,502
Yale	2,271
University of Pennsylvania	1,863
University of Michigan	1,762
Columbia	1,712
Northwestern	1,468
City University of New York	1,454
Princeton	1,404
University of Wisconsin	1,308

Harvard has an enrollment of some 15,000 to 16,000 students. New York University has about 35,000, or more than twice as many. And the University of Michigan's student body numbers some 40,000. This makes the percentage of Harvard-processed executives rather impressive.

It is not that you have to study so hard. The men and

women who win top academic honors seldom make it to the top in business. They tend to be rigid, tense, and distant with their colleagues, whereas those who just scraped by as students are competent and adaptable and relate well to other people. No, the reason for the overwhelming preponderance of executives with Harvard in their background stems from the incontrovertible fact that in most cases it is not what you know but whom you know that counts. And for generations Harvard has been the preferred institution of learning for the sons of the rich and powerful. This is where young people meet the other young people who will be useful or helpful to them later on. The halo effect is also at work here.

Uric acid is a better indication of a person's prospects for success than any horoscope reading. Uric acid is the villain in gout, that painful inflammatory disease, which used to be considered the wages of overindulgence in rich food and wine. Now researchers see gout as an indication of above-average intelligence. Men with high levels of uric acid tend to be successful in whatever they tackle.

Teeth are another indication. "I can walk into any big corporation and tell you who's on the way to the top," says one eminent oral surgeon. "He's about forty or fifty-five and his jaw muscles are as strong as an ox's because that guy is gritting his teeth too much. I just watch that telltale muscle in the cheek." Dentists uniformly testify that the men and women who suffer from bruxism (gritting or gnashing the teeth) are among their most prosperous and successful patients.

Marriage is one of the areas in which the difference between men and women is most manifest. And I don't mean that in the old-fashioned sense of *"Vive la différence!"* A study of six thousand men between the ages of forty-five and fifty-four revealed that the most successful of these men were married, most of them to their first wives—and that the marriages were dull.

It is quite another story for women. A woman who wants to get to the top might do better to remain single. Very few husbands can adapt themselves to a wife who brings home work five nights a week or has to fly to the Coast over the weekend to settle a contract dispute or evaluate a new factory site.

And husbands definitely do not accommodate themselves to a businesswoman's entertaining needs the way a wife does to her husband's. Few men are ready to play second fiddle at business dinners or move to another city because their wife's promotion involves a transfer. Marriage by and large is a drag on a woman who wants to succeed in business. Women who want to make it to the top and also want to be married must be prepared for plenty of flak on the domestic front—and possibly some heartbreak.

Not all of those people who want to succeed in business match this profile. What if you are the youngest or middle child? If you grew up happy? If your parents were poor—and content? What if you don't suffer from gout or grit your teeth? What if you (female) are happily married? Or (male) not at all?

You can still succeed in business.

The truth is that the psychological tools outlined in these chapters will be far more helpful to you than gout or going to Harvard—or even a dull marriage. The first eleven rules for success are:

1. Increase Your Success Potential.
2. Total Commitment.
3. Learn How to Learn What You Need to Know.
4. Synchronize Your Most Demanding Work with Your Body Clock.
5. Make Use of the Halo Effect.
6. Take Advantage of Your Flow State.
7. Capitalize on Other People's Inertia.

8. Divide and Conquer Opposition.
9. Learn How to Flatter.
10. Make Use of an "Old Boy (Girl) Network."
11. Find Yourself a Sponsor.

The twelfth rule is to use a psychological tool that may be the most valuable instrument for success that you will ever possess. You can use it to succeed in business, to become famous, rich, powerful, to gain love—almost anything. I call it

THE UNIQUE CLUSTER THEORY

When I was a graduate student in psychology at Columbia University, Professor Paffenberger was a man I admired tremendously. And I was not alone in my admiration. Professor Paffenberger was an inspiration as well as a beloved mentor to hundreds of doctoral candidates over the years. When he retired, his former students honored him at a farewell dinner. It was a sentimental occasion with many fond reminiscences. At the end of the evening, our guest of honor said, "I have one thing I want to pass on to you, one thing that I have learned over the years.

"If I had it to do over again," he told us, "I would concentrate on one small part of one subject and become the world's greatest authority on it."

I have never forgotten this. Having an area of expertise that no one else has gives a person a head start on success not only in the academic and professional fields, but in the business or almost any other world. The quality of uniqueness is the key. Over the years I have formulated my own adaptation of Professor Paffenberger's principle, the Unique Cluster Theory. And that is the twelfth and probably most important rule I can give you.

12.   Make Yourself Unique.

One can be unique because one knows more about a given subject than any other person in the world. One can also be unique because one knows more about a unique cluster of subjects than any other person.

I do not mean that the world's only auto mechanic, Greek scholar, and pomologist is going to make a million—although, who knows? There just might be a call for that cluster of skills. No, I am thinking of the television journalist who has a legal degree and has concentrated on foreign intelligence operations; of the realtor who is an expert on eighteenth-century American furniture and has a degree in landscaping.

I think of the young man who made a fortune in video-computer games, a prime example of the value of cultivating a unique cluster of skills. He invested $500 in manufacturing and marketing these games. Within a year, his sales had topped the $100-million mark. Explaining his runaway success, he said, "Not many people have the obscure combination of an engineering education, knowledge of video syntheses, and a background of work in an amusement park. I do. Add to that a course in economics in college and a sense of how the financial system works and you get success."

The more you can bring more than one facet or talent to a job or profession, the greater your probability of success. It is important to understand that you can make yourself unique. You can work to acquire a cluster of skills that no one else has. It is up to you.

There are other rules for success—all of them psychologically shrewd. They have worked for the most successful men and women. They will work for you.

13. Be Open to People.

"We can meet a total stranger and know in seconds whether that person does or does not want to spend more time with us," says Dr. Stephen Barrett, a psychiatrist who has compared the people who get the good things of life, who succeed, with those who do not. In general, he has found that "people who get lucky breaks handed to them by other people are those whose communication field is inviting and comfortable. Thomas Watson, the fabulously successful head of IBM, used to tell his salesmen, "If you don't genuinely like your customer, the chances are that he won't buy."

14. Be Persistent.

Never let well enough alone. A stockbroker follows the advice that her father gave her the day she started her first job. "Make one more call, my daddy told me," she said. "And I always do. I never leave my office at night without making one more call, doing one more thing. After I've cleared my desk and packed my briefcase, I sit down and make that one more call. Every single night. It pays off. Because of the time difference between the East and West Coasts, West Coast brokerage offices are open three hours after most people in New York have left for the day. I make a lot of money calling people in Los Angeles in that 'after hours' period," she said.

15. Trust Your Hunches.

One of the most successful businessmen I have met says that the only times he has made mistakes were when he did not trust his hunches. "I remember one time," he said, "I was offered a deal. The other guy was going to supply me with parts I needed at a very good price. But I didn't want to sign the contract. I didn't know why. But I didn't feel right about it. However, there was no basis for my feeling. No logic. So I went ahead and signed on the dotted line. And lost my shirt.

"The other guy was in big trouble with *his* suppliers. Deliveries of raw materials were late. So his deliveries were late. And the quality was spotty. There were all kinds of problems. I could have sued, but it would have been throwing good money after bad. I should have followed my hunch."

He should have. Hunches are a kind of subterranean logic shorthand. My friend had probably heard something about the man with whom he was going into the business deal. Perhaps through indirect channels. Or there may have been telltale physical signs in the man's demeanor—nervousness, eye blinking, knuckle cracking, an air of anxiety, that kind of thing. His subconscious was aware of these trouble signs and warned him not to go through with the deal. But he relied on logic—and lost his shirt.

The problem is that logic is not logical when a key factor is not included in the calculations. Hunches are usually based on facts filed away just below the conscious level.

Warning! Do not confuse your hunches with wishful thinking. This is the road to disaster.

16. Be Honest.

This may seem like superfluous advice, but there are too many people who believe that one cannot succeed without resorting to sharp practices or downright dishonesty. This feeling is reflected in the phrase "Nice guys finish last," which happens to be untrue. In a survey of top American executives who were asked very confidentially which one quality they considered most essential for success, honesty was the quality cited by almost every man. "Integrity" and "honesty" were the two words used over and over.

17. Be Flexible.

Only a decade ago, job-hopping was frowned upon. At that time, the American Institute of Management found that of 2,000 presidents of top corporations, 1,000 had spent their whole business career in the same corporation. The man who stuck with one firm, it turned out, had twice as good a chance of making it to the top as the man who worked for two firms. And six times the chance of the man who worked for four.

Today things are much different. Most men in the top executive ranks shifted from company to company until they found the firm and the job that best suited their talents and their ambitions. This makes a lot of sense. These men know a lot more about themselves and their capabilities after having matched themselves against men and situations in different companies. They have also picked up a lot of knowledge of different procedures, outlooks, expectations. And met more people who can be of help to them.

Most young men on their way up the corporate ladder these days tend to move every two or three years until they reach management level. In the twenty-six years (that's the average time) before a man becomes president of a company, he will make seven geographic moves and eleven moves up the ladder.

This may not hold true for women. The fact is that as I write this, we just do not know if women on their way up do—or will—move as often and to such good advantage as men.

There is one job change, however, that many women have to make that men do not. A man can start as mail boy and work his way up, but the woman who starts as receptionist and wants to work her way up always has to battle the lingering halo effect of that first job.

Polly started as a pool typist in an ad agency. She won several promotions on the basis of very hard work and the production of imaginative, hard-selling ad copy. But everyone still thought of her as Polly, the pool typist. She was the one asked to get coffee during brainstorming sessions. The only way she could overcome that halo effect was to move to another job. She became vice-president in charge of advertising for a bank. No one in the bank hierarchy knew her except as Polly, the brilliant advertising chief. As one management specialist puts it, "Women may have to move out before they can move in."

18.   Set Your Goals for Success.

Make a program, a step-by-step plan with short-term goals that will lead you to your ultimate goal.

As a rough guide, bear in mind that from twenty to thirty you should concentrate on finding the right field for your talents. At thirty, you should take time to assess what you have done and make plans for the next decade. Write down just what you want to accomplish over the next ten years—what you want to earn, what title you want to achieve, what living style you want. And then work to attain those goals.

Forty is the time for another assessment or reassessment. This can be a dangerous age—more dangerous, usually, for men than for women. Men get discouraged, some of them. They fear the onset of age. And some men, too many, go to pieces. Wreck their lives and their marriages. Screw up on their jobs. Psychologists and psychiatrists have a heavy case load of men in their forties.

If your forty-year stocktaking shows that your basic goals have changed, consider adjusting your life to meet your new goals. But proceed carefully. Use the Quick List Technique. And always keep in mind that the decade from forty to fifty can be dangerous. Be careful you don't burn your bridges behind you.

Otherwise, the years from forty to fifty are the time to consolidate the progress you have made, to solidify your position. It is the time to reach out for the power and the status that you are ready for, that you have earned.

And it helps to remember that men and women who expect to succeed usually fulfill their own great expectations.

19. Make Yourself at Home with Success.

Men and women who are confident of their abilities are more likely to succeed than those who lack confidence, even though the latter may be much more competent and talented and industrious. So it is important to make yourself believe that you will succeed.

Even before you reach your goal, treat yourself to success symbols. If you see yourself wearing diamond stud earrings or gold cuff links, carrying an expensive wallet or an impressive briefcase when you are a successful executive, treat yourself to these symbols today, whatever they are. They will make you feel successful here and now. They will also let other people know that you are successful. This is just one more way of making yourself at home with success.

Spend time thinking about what your life will be like when you have made it to the top. Daydream a little. See yourself in that executive suite with all the perquisites and power that go with it. Then think backward. Think of all the stages you have gone through on your way to the executive suite. All the lesser goals that you attained and then surpassed. Daydream about the lesser goals ahead and how they will feel when you reach them. All this will help you feel comfortable and at home with each new level that you reach—and be more effective.

There is another daydreaming technique that is also effective. It is known as programmed visualization and can help anyone who can set aside ten undisturbed minutes a day. The technique is simplicity itself.

The first step is to picture yourself as a success. You may see yourself in an impressive office, for instance, or in a boardroom where several high-powered executives are hanging on your every word.

The second step is to close your eyes and relax and try to see this picture in your mind as clearly as you can. Visualize yourself as a success for ten minutes, keeping your eyes closed. Your mind may wander and the picture disappear. If it does, don't worry, just focus on the picture again. The picture or details of the picture may change. This means that the intuitive half of your brain, the right side, is correcting your picture of success, making it more realistic.

After a week or so of this programmed visualization, you will find that you have begun to change certain of your attitudes or actions. You may become more decisive or less abrupt, more relaxed or less aloof. Whatever the changes, they represent the guidance of the intuitive side of your brain, gently leading you to the success you visualize and want.

20. Make Yourself Visible.

You will never be promoted, never considered for executive status, never made head of a management committee if no one knows you are there. Make sure people know who you are and what you do. But don't be pushy about it. That can create a negative halo effect.

One good road to visibility is volunteer work. Bill Green won a big promotion partly on the basis of a story that appeared in the newspaper. It went something like this:

FUND-RAISING GOAL TOPPED

William R. Green, Jr., assistant sales manager for the ABCD Firm of this city, who served as chairman of the Destitute Fathers Society fund-raising committee, announced that the committee had topped its goal of $100,000 by $15,000. This is a record in fund-raising for the society.

"The committee was as effective a group of people as I have ever worked with," Green said. "Every one of them went over his quota. Sam Brown, Mary White, Sally Blue, Ned Turquoise and Len Orange all contributed time and energy above and beyond the call of duty."

Bill looked good on three counts here. First, he raised a record amount of money for an important local charity. Second, he praised the people he worked with and named each one of them, which made them well disposed toward him. And third, he made sure that the reporter included the name of his firm. This was good publicity for the firm—and ensured that the story would come to the notice of management.

Another way to become known without stepping on your colleagues' toes, or sensibilities, is to join a professional society in your field—and play an active role in it. This will bring you not only to the attention of your own management, but to that of top executives in other companies in the same field.

21. Think Negatively.

There may be power in positive thinking, but when it comes to succeeding in business, it is important to learn how to worry constructively. This means looking ahead at every step of the game to see what might go wrong—and figuring out what to do if it does. It is impossible to foresee every eventuality, but you have probably heard of Murphy's Law: If anything can go wrong, it will. Let that be your guide. The successful individual is the one who does his worrying in advance. When a problem arises, chances are he has already worried out a solution for it.

22. Learn to Make Decisions.

Decision making can be learned. It is a matter of confidence and practice. And above all, of competence and know-how. No one can make a decision on the basis of ignorance. So the first rule for effective decision making is to master your job, your subject, whatever it is. And the second rule is to practice. Start out by making a list of the decisions you make in the course of a single day. Whether to sleep ten minutes later; whether to walk to work or take the bus; whether to join the tennis club, where you will get to know your neighbors better, or subscribe to the ballet, where you will meet your boss and his wife. You probably did not devote a whole lot of thought to these decisions. And if it turned out that you were wrong, you don't lie awake at night and fret about it.

With practice, you can transfer this easy decision making to the big decisions. And the way to do this is to make another list—a list of the decisions you had to make in the course of the week that you considered important. At the end of the week, take a look at your list. How did you do? Would you change your mind on any of these? Why? Do you know something now that you did not know then? Was there any way you could have known that fact or facts at the time you had to make the decision? If there was no way you could have known it, then put it out of your mind. If the answer is yes, then you have learned something. You have spotted a personal weakness. Now that you are aware of it, you can correct this weakness. Next time you have to make a similar decision, you will be in command of all the necessary facts.

And that is all there is to it. After a couple of months, you should find that you are handling major decisions as easily and quickly as the minor ones.

23. Put Yourself First.

Just remember, no one else will. You must keep your own interests and goals firmly in mind—and work to achieve them.

24. Learn How to Negotiate.

See Chapter Seventeen.

25. Learn How to Handle People.

See Chapter Seventeen.

And no, it does not help to marry the boss's daughter. The young man who marries the girl next door reaches the top in business in an average of twenty-six years; the young man who marries the boss's daughter usually takes twenty-five years and ten months. We are all aware of exceptions to this rule, of instant promotions, but they are truly few and far between. And often are fleeting. In a change of management, the boss's son-in-law's head is usually among the first to roll.

And as for marrying the boss's son, forget it. That is no way for a woman to succeed in business. You will have to wait for your father-in-law to die and then **for** your husband to die or become incapacitated before you get your chance to show what you can do. That is too long to hang around wasting your time and your good mind.

CHAPTER TWELVE

The Wealth Seeker

Two key questions about money. The single-minded Wealth Seekers. Why most of them know very little about their motivations. The fulfilling treadmill.

While there is hardly a person in this world who is not interested in money—oh, possibly a guru here and there on a Himalayan peak—there are very few—very, very few—people for whom money is the ultimate goal in life. Most of us want more money than we have, because our needs tend to escalate and inflation nips at our economic heels. A high salary or generous income may be one of the comforting, pleasant, and exciting by-products of the goals we set ourselves, but it is rarely the ultimate goal.

How can you tell if money is truly your ultimate goal? Can you be sure? Yes, you can. Your answers to the two key questions below can establish immediately whether or not you are a Wealth Seeker, a person who wants money more than anything else in the world. The questions should be answered yes or no without hesitation. Do not stop to ponder your responses. You may be surprised at what your answers reveal about you.

1. Are you positive that money is what you want more than anything else in the world?
2. Do you plan to change your life-style when you make your fortune and indulge your desires for travel, jewels, a beautiful home, expensive automobiles, a fabulous wardrobe, the best of everything?

If you answered yes to the first question and yes to the second question, you are not a Wealth Seeker. If you answered no to the first question and no to the second question, you are not a Wealth Seeker. If you answered no to the first question and yes to the second question, you are not a Wealth Seeker.

The Wealth Seeker will answer yes to the first question and no to the second. The true Wealth Seeker has absolutely no doubt that money is what he or she wants more than anything else in the world. No Quick List testing is needed to help such people know what they want. They know. They have always known, as far back as they can remember.

The Wealth Seeker is so sure about his goal that he does not need to take this mini-quiz. The real purpose of these two key questions is to help those people for whom money is *not* the ultimate goal to understand that they are confusing the end with the means. These people should go back to the Quick List Technique and spend more time determining their real goal. Money is not it.

The individual whose ultimate goal is riches has absolutely no hesitancy in responding negatively to the second question. The person who answers yes, who has plans for a more luxurious life-style and a whole shopping list of goodies he intends to acquire once he has the means, reveals that he has other ultimate goals, that money is a subgoal. He may want luxury. He may want to travel to exotic places. He may want to build his own spaceship. He may want (or think he wants) to spend the rest of his life on a perpetual vacation. If so, these desires represent his true goal. Not money. Money is simply the commodity that makes the goal possible.

The Wealth Seeker, on the other hand, wants money for money's sake. To him, it is desirable in itself— something to count, something to handle, something to amass and never let go.

To most people, money is a form of frozen energy. Liquefied, it provides security, pleasure, and comfort; helps others; makes the world a better place. It can be used for a host of selfish and unselfish purposes. But there are some people for whom money is an end in itself. The person who wants money more than anything else is a quite different breed of cat from the one who wants to succeed in business or achieve fame or power. For the latter, money may be a single important or un-important facet of the ultimate goal; for the former, it is everything.

The pursuit of riches sentences an individual to one of life's treadmills. It is truly a treadmill, because it is psychologically impossible for most Wealth Seekers to stop the pursuit, to say, "That's enough. I am as rich as I want to be." There is no end to the riches they want to acquire.

But they have sentenced themselves to that treadmill, and they do not find it monotonous because they are doing what they want. The monotony is in the eye of the beholder. Research has shown that people are at their personal best, their most fulfilled, while they are working toward their goal. Not when they achieve it. Achievement often results in a letdown. So since the Wealth Seeker never reaches his goal, he may experi-ence a high degree of his special form of fulfillment, be happier, and have more fun than most of the rest of the population.

If you are a Wealth Seeker, you will learn more about yourself in the following chapter, about characteristics and motivations that you may never have suspected you possessed than you ever knew before. Wealth Seekers are among the least introspective of individuals. Learning about yourself will help you understand your strengths and weaknesses. This self-knowledge should help you exercise your innate talents to accumulate those riches you seek.

CHAPTER THIRTEEN

The Driving Force

The cookie-cutter people. The rags-to-riches syndrome. How big is a dollar bill? The secret of making money. The multimillionaire who dined in cafeterias. The dollar haircut. Emeralds and brown-bag lunches. Why they want to be rich, rich, RICH! The poor little child within. The validity of money as a goal.

The individual routes to wealth are myriad—and yet almost startling in their similarity. And so are the men and women who are driven to amass riches. They are thin and fat, short and tall, white and black and yellow and red, endomorphs and ectomorphs and mesomorphs. But psychologically, they could have been stamped out by the same cookie cutter.

An extraordinarily high percentage of self-made multimillionaires come from a background of poverty. There is nothing so surprising about this rags-to-riches pattern. A psychologist would be surprised only if the pattern did *not* exist. Just as sex looms as such an overpowering drive because our sex needs are not satisfied as systematically as are our other prepotent needs, the drive to accumulate money can be overwhelmingly powerful for someone who grew up poor. Money even *looks* bigger to poor people. In one study in which people were asked to estimate the size of a dollar bill, the poorest group consistently saw it as larger than life size, while middle- and high-income participants came very close to estimating the actual size.

Education is not an important factor in amassing wealth. As often as not, it is the man who has gone no further than the first or second year of high school who makes the fortune. "I was too dumb to know that what I was doing was impossible," said one man who had built up an immense fortune.

These men are audacious. They take gambles that other men would not touch with a ten-foot pole and work like galley slaves to make them pay off. A financial journalist who has observed the rich for more than a decade says, "None of the self-made rich I've ever met seemed to be stupid and just lucky." They are smart. Shrewd. They can spot trends, foresee needs; their genius lies in knowing how to make money out of other people's ideas. This is the real secret in making money—capitalizing on the creative thinking of others and turning it to practical use.

These men and women are finely tuned to other people. Very perceptive. They observe other people. They know how to respond to others to get what they want. And they know how others react to them.

When they meet someone, they ask themselves questions like "Is he signaling me that he is receptive? Or is he signaling that he is negative? Am I going to have to use reverse psychology on him? Is he secure? Or insecure? What is the best way of handling him? What is the key to this man? What does he want? Or need? And how can I supply it?"

The passion for money replaces human needs. "It's a question of desire," says a man who founded a nationwide motel chain, a typical Wealth Seeker who grew up poor and dropped out of school at the age of fourteen.

"You've got to have that push, that drive," he says. "You've got to be hungry.

"I'm always trying to make a deal or sell somebody something or trying to get somebody to do something I want to do," the motel magnate says. "I don't know of anything else I'd rather be doing. The guy who works only eight hours a day and doesn't take any risks is a guy who will trade everything he's got for a little bit of security."

It is not a "little bit of security" that the Wealth Seekers are after, but a whole lot of money. And the process of accumulating it is everything. The more money they have, the more omnipotent they feel—even if they do nothing whatsoever with that money except use it to make still more money. No matter how much wealth these men and women accumulate, they never have enough. They always feel deprived.

One of the richest men in this country, a man who was born "dirt-poor," he says, a man who made his first big money in oil, still lives in the same house he bought thirty-odd years ago when he was an oil-field roustabout. The only outward evidence that this man has more money than his blue-collar neighbors is his office. He converted his garage into an office that is equipped with the latest communications equipment, and there he spends fourteen to sixteen and sometimes more hours a day wheeling and dealing on American, European, and Asian stock exchanges. He picks up the telephone to call Zurich or Tokyo as casually as most men make a golf date.

Not all the men who have made riches their goal in life—and have accumulated vast wealth—are quite this frugal, but inside each and every one of them there is still that poor little boy who promised himself that one day he was going to be richer than anyone else. Rich beyond belief.

One of these was a man who ran up a fortune of more than a hundred million dollars and in middle age became a world-famous art collector. He thought nothing of paying thousands and thousands of dollars to acquire a single sculpture or painting. He thought of his works of art as marvelous investments. He liked to talk about his Horatio Alger ascent from poverty.

"I tasted poverty as a child," he said, "and I made up my mind that I was never going to go hungry again." He never did. But neither did he indulge himself in lobster or caviar or thick, tender steaks or fine wines. His idea of a splendid meal was the blue-plate special at the cafeteria down the street from his skyscraper suite of offices. The poor little boy inside, the one who had sworn never to go hungry again, still did not feel that he could afford anything more extravagant than the cafeterias that had dazzled him with their rich abundance when he was a hungry child.

Rags-to-riches is by no means an exclusively American phenomenon. A European multimillionaire, who started working at the age of twelve as a laundry boy, then went on to be a street-corner flower vendor, a pushcart peddler, and a garage attendant, became a real estate tycoon who controlled great parcels of income-producing properties—parking garages, hotels, motels, residential complexes, shopping centers, and office buildings—by the time he was forty. This man, who is worth at least $300 million, spends his vacation in Communist Europe—because it is cheap. He boasts about the $1 haircuts he gets in the Rumanian resort he patronizes.

I have talked about men here, because the great majority of people who have earned their own enormous fortunes have been men. But women also have traveled the rags-to-riches route. One woman who made a fantastic fortune in cosmetics was one of the stingiest souls who ever lived. She used to take her lunch to her office in a brown-paper bag. She had a weakness for fine gems, but even when she was bedecked with emeralds, the specter of poverty and hunger never left her.

Psychological portraits of individuals who seek wealth reveal a sense of isolation, of loneliness, of the hungry-for-love little child within. Does this mean that Wealth Seekers should make an effort to change their goal? To work for fame or success in business or politics? Absolutely not. These would be artificial goals. That would not be what they want more than anything else in the world. They want money. And the making of money is an utterly absorbing pursuit. It gives the Wealth Seekers more satisfaction, more downright pleasure than anything else. And it is what they should do.

CHAPTER FOURTEEN

The Road to Riches

Why yesterday's road to riches is today's dead end. The Major Five and the Minor Seven guidelines. Money's orgasmic potential. The dangers of crowd psychology. Why you should not work for anyone.

Andrew Carnegie, the nineteenth-century steel tycoon, used to tell young men who sought his advice, "Put all your eggs in one basket. And watch that basket. That's the way to make money." In this age of brutal taxation, dwindling natural resources, and rapid change, committing all one's eggs to one basket is more likely to prove an Open Sesame to bankruptcy. Accumulating wealth is a far more complicated feat than it was two or three generations ago. But it can be done. It has been done.

As the title of this chapter hints, there is just one road to riches. Although it may seem that the individual routes to wealth are myriad, the fact is that they are as much alike as Southern California's freeways. And no wonder. People who share the same psychological profile can be expected to employ the same means to attain the goal that they have in common.

The fortunes of the self-made rich come from diverse sources—precious metals, real estate, oil, inventions, services, shrewd investments, one thousand and one combinations of these and other sources—but the ways the Wealth Seekers seize upon the potential of these sources and turn them into solid cash are practically identical.

As one entrepreneur explained, "It's basically a matter of borrowing four dollars and buying one X. You sell that X for eight dollars. You use the four dollars you have earned to buy another X, which you sell for eight dollars. And then you take that eight dollars and buy two X's, which you sell for sixteen dollars—and so on."

But what I want to give you is psychological guidelines, because your attitude and the way you channel your inner drives are far more important than knowing that you need money to make money. Wealth Seekers seem to carry that knowledge in their bones. It is second nature to them. But these psychological guidelines are even more basic. You can use them no matter whether you plan to make your money in farm widgets or in fashion. There are five major and seven minor guidelines.

THE MAJOR FIVE

1. Make Money Your Mistress.

Do not waste time and energy on sex. You will discover that making money is more orgasmic than sex in the long run. This is no empty promise. Men have reported that they have become stimulated to the point of ejaculation in thinking about or consummating a favorable contract or a big sale. Some have reported that they routinely have an erection when stimulated by the prospect of a big deal. "I can even get an erection talking with one of my brokers on the telephone," one Wealth Seeker told me. "Especially if he's telling me about getting in on a good thing."

2. Find a Need and Fill It.

The Wealth Seeker's great talent is that of spotting trends and foreseeing needs. Henry Ford's Model T automobile filled the need for cheap, dependable transportation. And so, after the Second World War, did the Volkswagen Beetle. The coast-to-coast fast-food chains are another example of meeting a need. So are supermarkets, motels, best sellers, televised football games, contraceptive devices, and frozen orange juice. The people who discover and meet needs most efficiently and imaginatively are the ones who make fortunes.

There are always new needs. Probably the most publicized group of contemporary Horatio Alger heroes who have made the rags-to-riches trip in the past decade are the entertainers—the rock singers, the television stars, the sports figures. Their faces are almost as familiar to us as the one we see in the bathroom mirror every morning. They make big money. But the men and women who make even bigger money are the agents and managers and packagers and publicists who provide the services and know-how and the vehicles the entertainers need. To these people, the entertainers are what iron ore was to Andrew Carnegie: raw material to be processed and marketed—profitably.

3. Beware of Crowd Psychology.

Nearly a century ago, a French physician, Gustav le Bon, observed that "When people are transformed into a crowd, they possess a sort of collective mind, which makes them feel, think, and act in a manner quite different from that in which each one of them would feel, think, and act were he in a solitary state. The sense of responsibility that always controls individuals," he noted, "disappears entirely in a crowd."

He was correct. And when it comes to matters of money, crowd psychology can be disastrous. Not too long ago, there was a meeting of top financial experts, the men in charge of investing the funds of the country's largest financial institutions. At this meeting, these shrewd specialists concluded that airlines were the most promising investment around, and they placed a significant percentage of the funds of the institutions they represented in airline stocks. During the next twelve months, these stocks plunged a sickening 75 percent.

What had happened? An unexpected reverse of some sort? A disaster? No. The indications of weakness in these stocks had been there twelve months earlier for those willing to see them. What had happened was that these men fell victim to crowd psychology and invested in an industry that, if each of them had evaluated it on his own, he would not have touched with a ten-foot pole.

Yale psychologist Irving Janis studied the phenomenon of group think and came to the same conclusion that Gustav le Bon had reached before him. In group situations, Professor Janis found, individuals display "mindless conformity and collective misjudgment of serious risks, which are collectively laughed off in a clubby atmosphere of relaxed conviviality."

The man or woman who wants to make money more than anything else in the world cannnot afford to be a victim of crowd psychology. Not only is the crowd usually wrong, but even if it is right, there is usually little profit in following it. It is the leaders who skim the financial cream off a given situation, not the followers.

This does not mean that you should reject information input. The more input the better. But the fact that a number of highly respected experts suddenly decide that the wave of the future lies in plastic ice cream cones is no reason for you to believe that they know something you don't. You must have the guts to back your own analytical judgments and keep a psychological distance that will enable you to appraise the collective judgments of others instead of being caught up in a thoughtless collective *mis*judgment. It is no happenstance that most self-made multimillionaires are also loners.

4. Be the Boss.

The man who makes the fortune is the employer, not the employee. Some money-oriented men and women will settle—and quite happily—for the huge salaries paid to top executives these days. With bonuses and perquisites, the yearly take ranges close to the million-dollar level for the favored handful at the top. But these men are not Wealth Seekers. Their goal is success or power. And the Wealth Seeker is rarely if ever found in this group. His loner tendencies make him uncomfortable in the corporate structure.

He is better off being boss, even if only of a staff of one—himself. He will work harder for himself than for any corporate structure. And he will make more money than any corporation will pay him.

5. Develop Your Manipulating Skills.

Most people consider the idea of manipulating others, getting them to do what you want them to, rather distasteful. The fact is, however, that we all manipulate people at one time or another without even being conscious of it. Wealth Seekers tend to manipulate intuitively and are quite adept at the art, but there are ways and means of manipulation that you may not have discovered or that do not come naturally to you. They can be learned. See Chapter Seventeen.

THE MINOR SEVEN

Many of the rules for succeeding in business are equally valid as guidelines along the road to riches—especially the seven listed below, which were outlined in Chapter Eleven.

Never Let Well Enough Alone.
Trust Your Hunches.
Be Honest.
Be Flexible.
Learn to Make Decisions.
Think Negatively.
Put Yourself First.

I do not want to give the impression that every Wealth Seeker will achieve great riches if he or she corresponds to the psychological profile I sketched in the previous chapter and makes use of the twelve guidelines given here. No such guarantees are possible in this uncertain world of ours. Personal factors such as physical health, stress tolerance, and stamina quotient play a part, as well as virtually unpredictable political, social, and economic factors that can thwart even the most single-mindedly daring Wealth Seeker. But I do believe that individuals who sincerely want money more than anything else in the world and who use the psychological tools I have provided will end up with more money than most people. And that most of them will end up with a lot more money.

CHAPTER FIFTEEN

The Power Drive

How Conrad achieved political power. When power is inherited. Richard's breakthrough to power. The power class and the status-symbol wife. The power person's automobile image. Affiliatives and Dominant Loners.

"Power" is a loaded word in our society. It makes people uncomfortable. Somehow it is not quite "nice." And yet everyone wants a degree of power—to be able to get what he wants and to make others do what he wants them to do, which is all that power really is, at least some of the time.

This section is for those men and women whose goal in life is power. And always has been. Other people, however, who simply want a degree or two more of power, can use the same insights and techniques to acquire the amount of power that makes them comfortable.

Women may actually be more power-hungry than men. Studies indicate that while they are in high school

and college, they pursue power goals far more energeti-
cally than male students. It is impossible to draw valid
conclusions from these findings, however, until follow-
up studies are done to see if the power drive is main-
tained over the years. Power has only recently become a
possibility for significant numbers of women. When
enough women achieve power, it is possible that they
may change the world—or they may adopt male power
patterns. It is too early to tell. One thing we do know,
and that is that the man or woman who is driven by the
need for power does not need any test to find out if
power is what he or she really wants. He knows. She
knows.

Conrad wanted political power. His father had served
several terms in the state legislature, and Conrad had
grown up with politics in the very air he breathed.
When he was old enough, his father took him along on
campaign trips. Conrad loved the excitement of cam-
paigning, the feeling of being on the inside, the sense of
power that his father and his colleagues exuded. And he
wanted it all.

In college, he studied hard enough to maintain re-
spectable marks, but his real interest was in the campus
political scene. As president of the student government,
he invited prominent city and state officials to speak at
the college. His great triumph was when one of the
state's senators to Washington addressed the student
body. The Senator, who knew Conrad's father and was
impressed by the young man's energy, told Conrad that
he had a spot for him in his Washington office when he
graduated. And that summer, he joined the Senator's
Washington staff as office boy, errand boy, and general
flunky. He made coffee, ran the duplicating machine,
typed letters, did research—and met hundreds of the
Senator's constituents.

After two years in Washington, he went back home,

enrolled in law school, and started creating a political base for himself. Shortly after he graduated from law school, he ran for the city council and won. Today, Conrad is a state senator, just as his father used to be. But he plans to run for the U.S. Senate when the time is ripe, and he is regarded as a man to watch. Even now, he has great power. His speeches, the positions he takes in the state legislature, his votes on issues influence the spending of hundreds of thousands of dollars and the quality of life of the residents of his state.

Ingrid did not have to seek power. She inherited it. Her father died when she was thirty and left her the sole owner of a vast international business empire. No one expected her to be more than a figurehead. And perhaps not even that. Her life had always been devoted to pleasure and excitement. She flew her own jet, skied like a maniac, was constantly in the gossip columns, her name linked with those of rich and famous men. Her father doted on her and was amused by her escapades. But then he died. And the scramble for power began.

Ingrid was the nominal head of the empire, but the power was in the hands of the director and the top executives in charge of day-to-day operations, all of them hungry for more money, more power—and sure they would get it. Ingrid had shown no interest in her inheritance. She was grief-stricken and, after acquiring a mourning wardrobe in Paris and Milan and New York, went into seclusion. She emerged to make occasional headlines when she attended a royal wedding and was involved in an automobile accident. The business went on, suffering from infighting and the lack of a leader. There were rumors of takeover efforts, from within and without.

And then Ingrid grasped the power she had inherited. The takeover maneuvers had shaken her. She was used to being the heiress, the beauty, the daredevil playgirl.

She suddenly realized that all her life she had enjoyed vicarious power. Her father's power had been hers. It had set the tone of her life. And now it was endangered.

It took less than a year for her to turn her empire around. She cleared out deadwood. She fired those executives who opposed her—men she had formerly deferred to, whose advice she had followed unquestioningly and unhesitatingly—and surrounded herself with vigorous young executives who were ready to break with the old ways that had worked for her father but were now outdated. She set the top executives whom she retained to work teaching her everything they knew. "She keeps pushing, pushing, pushing," one of them grumbled. "She wants to know how and why, the basis for every figure and fact."

Ingrid at thirty-five is completely in control of her empire. Today her name is in the financial pages, not the gossip columns, and she is referred to as "a shrewd gambler" and "a brilliant operator," no longer as "playgirl" and "spoiled heiress." Ingrid discovered that power is the ultimate excitement.

When one intrepid reporter asked if she planned to get married, Ingrid answered bluntly, "I could not respect a husband who was not my equal. And there are very few men today who are. Who else has as much power? Who else has as much money?"

Richard did not inherit power. Nor did he have a concrete goal the way Conrad did. But Richard always knew that he wanted to be boss. He was certainly the boss at home. As the oldest, he ordered his younger brothers around.

When he graduated from college, he went to work as a trainee in an advertising agency. Impressed by the amount of business the agency did with a copying firm, Richard decided there was more of a future for him with the copying firm.

He spent a year with the copying firm, then decided to start up on his own with $5,000 his grandmother had left him. It was a one-man operation. His profits were slim, and the hours were killing—but he was his own boss. His breakthrough to power came when a computer salesman suggested that he start thinking bigger, get more sophisticated machines and start offering simplified computer services to the firms he dealt with.

Within ten years, Richard was president of a computer-services firm employing more than one hundred people with offices on both coasts. This would be enough success for most people, but Richard wanted more. He expanded again, setting up a business-consulting service. His computer capability, his experience, and his conviction that he could plot a better future for almost any business were his stock in trade. This was the move that brought him power.

Today big corporations ask his advice about executives, about mergers, about stock issues. Government heads ask his recommendations for high positions, his advice in diversifying industry. Some say that he is more powerful than the heads of many small nations. A word from Richard can affect a country's credit in world markets, can topple a government, and certainly can affect the price of coffee.

Conrad's power consisted of getting others to do what they very often would not have done unless he had lobbied for a bill or won their votes by appealing to their idealism or self-interest, using what has been called the "strategy of human desire."

Ingrid controlled an enterprise that gave her a power base, the potential to wield power through awarding contracts, hiring workers, buying raw materials, and so on. People who possess power-bestowing resources—a business, energy sources, raw materials, control of a bank, landholdings—are often unaware of the power potential they possess until, like Ingrid, they are in danger of losing it and shocked to realize how much they have been taking for granted.

Richard, like Conrad, had always wanted power, but it took years and a great deal of work and accumulating of experience before he was in a position to exert real power. Part of his power resided in the fact that he made himself into an indispensable middleman, adept at manipulating businesses and governments. As his inside knowledge of corporations and countries increased, so did his strength as a power broker.

Conrad and Ingrid and Richard. Three very different people. All of them addicted to power. Is there a common denominator? A single psychological profile? Actually, yes. They are more alike than one might suppose. They possess the same power characteristics. They want to convince others. They take action to do this. They make an impact. And everything they do increases their prestige.

Power people fall into two categories—the Affiliatives and the Dominant Loners. They have certain characteristics in common. They are usually the eldest or only child. Their parents are middle or upper-middle class and always expected a lot of them, with the result that they were achievement-oriented very early. They wanted to please their parents more than other children their age. It used to be thought that the inner need for power stemmed from childhood feelings of inferiority or inadequacy, but research has shown that most power people had a sense of power even in childhood.

As they go through school, they are often voted class president and appointed to student-faculty committees. They are known for their ability to smooth over conflicts and negotiate compromises. They very seldom allow themselves to get upset—and when they are, they do their best not to show it. They are cool, capable.

As adults they feel most comfortable with other power people. In fact, they tend to think of themselves as a special class, choosing their friends and associates from other members of this power class.

An interesting sidelight on their personalities is their choice of automobiles. While they may invest in luxury cars—the Cadillacs, the Mercedes-Benzes, the Lincoln Continentals, the Rolls-Royces—for the halo effect, the cars they really like, that give them pleasure, are expensive sports cars. They like their maneuverability. And they prefer stick shifts, which give them more control over the machine.

This need to control is the key to the power personality. All the people in both groups are intensely manipulative, know how to play on the fears and desires of others to control them. The men see their families, and especially their wives, as status symbols. And they prefer their wives to stay at home, not to pursue careers or professions.

This may be changing. A recent survey of college men found that seniors with high power needs were more willing for their wives to work than their classmates were. But I would not jump to any hasty conclusions. It may be that a working wife will be tomorrow's status symbol.

Where the Affiliatives and the Dominant Loners differ is in personality traits and the way they employ power.

The Affiliatives are very much controlled. They are careful, although fast, drivers. They like people and they are joiners, belonging to the country club, trade associations, social clubs, political organizations. Their telephones are always ringing and they make a point of being available.

Affiliatives tend to use their power for the benefit of others—for a corporation, a university, even an underworld gang. They know how to get the most and best work out of people. They know how to delegate responsibilities. They get great pride out of the knowledge that they can make people work harder for them than anyone else can. But they pay for this power. It shortens their lives. A quarter of a century ago, researchers tested the power drive of a group of Harvard graduates who were in their thirties. A recent follow-up revealed that over half of them either had very high blood pressure—or had died from heart failure and other stress-related diseases.

The Dominant Loners, on the other hand, are single-minded, driving souls. They hate organizations. And if they have to operate within the framework of a corporation, they see to it that the people who work with them are directly responsible to them—not to the corporation. Unlike the Affiliatives, they tend to be impulsive. They are often described as "modern-day pirates," and they have the quality of ruthless daring and cynical charm associated with the men who used to sail the Spanish Main—for the pleasure of the profit.

How do Conrad, Ingrid, and Richard conform to this profile? Very neatly. It is almost like fitting pieces into a jigsaw puzzle.

Conrad is an Affiliative, and it shows in his annual physical checkups. His doctor has warned him about his blood pressure, prescribing tranquilizers for him upon occasion, and lectured him about the need for regular exercise.

Ingrid is more of a Dominant Loner. She rides roughshod over her executives, and she can be ruthless—as shown by her dismissal of men who had been associated with her father for many years. Like most Dominant Loners, she is uncomplicated; does not suffer from ulcers, high blood pressure; does not need sleeping pills or tranquilizers.

She is supremely self-confident; never questions herself or her judgment for a minute. She has a superb understanding of what makes other people tick. "She can sum up a man in a glance," one international businessman says.

Richard is part Affiliative, part Dominant Loner. He knows how to manage people, how to play on their fears as well as their desires. He pays attention to his health, exercises, watches his weight, does not drink or smoke; but he is nervous, tense as a coiled spring, and never satisfied with himself or others. At the same time, he is quite happy with his life. The sense of power gratifies him beyond description. There are times when he leans back in the luxurious leather armchair in his private jet on the way from one high-level conference to another and smiles to himself as he thinks of the effect he has on the world. An effect, he believes, that is for good.

Conrad, Ingrid, and Richard fit the classic power profile. The three of them use power constructively; are builders, not destroyers, forces for good, not evil. They have accepted the responsibilities of power.

But have they achieved their goal? One would think so, but the fact is that neither Richard nor Conrad will ever feel he has achieved ultimate power. Ingrid's concept of power is more limited. As long as she can exercise power over her empire, she is content.

CHAPTER SIXTEEN

How to Make People Do What You Want

The twelve-letter dirty word. Why everyone is susceptible to flattery. The importance of the stroking letter. High-level diplomatic flattery. How to make a person think you're taking him seriously. The only way to get a stubborn person to do what you want him to. Why you should help your opponent save face. The reward technique. And when you should not give rewards. How to get your husband to bring you coffee in bed. The theory of intermittent reinforcement. Why guilt works. And the antidote for guilt. How to use fear to clinch a sale. To size people up.

The ability to manipulate effectively is the key to power. Bertrand Russell, the philosopher, said that power is "the production of intended effects," which is just another way of saying "getting what you want." How does one produce those effects? By manipulating people and circumstances.

If "power" is a loaded word, not quite "nice," in our society, then "manipulation" is a twelve-letter dirty word. We condemn manipulative people—and yet we all manipulate. With varying degrees of skill and success. The secretary who insists that the executive calling her boss come onto the line before she puts her boss on the telephone; the executive who purposely arrives late for a business lunch; the mother who tells her two-year-old that it is time for juice and a cookie instead of saying, "Come in the house now. It's getting cold outside" are manipulating. There are a thousand and one ways to manipulate. Physical persuasion is one. If you punch someone in the nose, that person will probably agree to do whatever it is you want, but he won't like it. And there is a chance that he just might beat you to the punch. Physical persuasion is a clumsily primitive method of manipulation.

The power person achieves and increases his power by getting people to do what he wants them to *by making them want to do it*. And the most effective psychological tools to accomplish this are flattery, rewards, guilt, and fear—in that order.

FLATTERY

Everyone has an inferiority complex. We tend to consider successful or powerful individuals superior in many ways, but I have never met a successful or powerful person who truly felt superior. Without exception, such people fear that somebody will eventually find them out. Even though on one level they know exactly how powerful and successful they are, somewhere deep inside they do not quite believe it. This makes them susceptible to flattery.

There is a basic insecurity that prevents people from feeling pleased with themselves and their achievements and impels them to work to achieve success and power.

Take my friend Stan, a lawyer, who manages a group of television and recording stars and has built an entertainment empire, starting from nothing. Stan is immensely capable, has an impressive track record of success, and yet he told me that when he met with a group of bankers to discuss financing for film projects, he was so nervous that his hands were clammy. "I was absolutely terrified," he said. "Here am I, this little guy asking for a couple of million, and here are all these big-deal bankers." Stan could have bought and sold those men in the conference room twice over. His inferiority complex was at work.

People have told me after I have made a television appearance or given a lecture, when they see me with my hair done, my makeup on, "Oh, you are so competent. It must be great to be so organized, so calm, cool, and collected." I am always tremendously pleased—but at the same time I wonder what they would say on those days when I'm frantic and falling apart. When I am behind with my column; when the lift comes off my heel and I'm late for the hairdresser. Most of the time I am cool, calm, and collected. But that's not the Joyce that I know best. I know the woman who is often harassed, whose desk is piled high—and who needs the attentions of the hairdresser.

So when you tell someone that he or she is marvelous, talented, successful, handsome, effective, brilliant, well dressed, vigorous, that person is going to lap it up. Even the most successful and powerful individuals need to be stroked, told how great they are. And those people who are less successful, less powerful appreciate the stroking even more. So much that they will probably be delighted to do anything they can for the person who strokes them.

The key to successful flattery is to zero in on those areas of real concern to the person being flattered—her new car, his promotion, his daughter's history prize—or to bolster his ego in areas where he may feel unsure— "That was a great speech, J.C. You had them in the palm of your hand"; or "That was a masterly memo. You summed up a tricky situation very clearly"; or "I was impressed with the way you handled Neil's resignation. It could have been a sticky affair." The man who has quietly lost fifteen pounds without ever once talking about his diet will be pleased if you compliment him on how well he looks. This is one of the few appearance compliments you can give a man.

Secondhand flattery is tremendously effective. Things like "Greg told me that everybody over at your shop is excited about this new campaign you worked out. You must feel pretty good about it. Congratulations." This bolsters the ego, lets him know you think he's a great guy—and that his co-workers do too. It is a good feeling to know that people are talking about you in favorable terms.

Flattery is not confined to compliments. Using someone's name several times in a conversation is flattering to that person—if you are his superior. Referring to something an individual said at a previous encounter is flattering. He gets the message that you listened carefully to what he said and remembered it.

Many executives put aside a few minutes every day to write what one company president calls "stroking" letters to friends and business acquaintances who have received promotions or awards or delivered a speech or gotten married. The recipient's opinion of you rises because he feels that you have a high opinion of him. Write your stroking letters by hand, unless your penmanship is so atrocious that the strokee will not be able to decipher it. In that case, type your stroking note and be sure to make a couple of mistakes just to underline the fact that you cared enough to do it yourself.

Former Secretary of State Kissinger was a skilled practitioner of flattery in his diplomatic negotiations. "You must be very subtle," he explains. "Most national leaders are extremely shrewd. They have a high resistance to being manipulated; they manipulate others. You have to treat a highly intelligent man as a highly intelligent man. You must make him immediately aware that you are taking him very seriously. And you must enhance his confidence. Flattery is simply to make a man believe he can solve his problems."

Listening, not imitation, may be the sincerest form of flattery. Most people don't listen. They simply wait out another person's speech or comment, planning just what they are going to say when he stops talking. The result is a series of monologues instead of an exchange of views.

If you want to influence someone, listen to what he says. Don't just sit there alert for the flaws in his argument that you can use against him later. Listen. What is he trying to tell you? What is it that *he* wants? When he finishes talking, ask him about any points that you do not understand. Then tell him what it is you want and point out the areas where you are in agreement and those where you do not agree. He will be flattered that you have listened intently, that you take him seriously, and that you truly want to understand his position.

The sensitive-listening technique, which I described in Chapter Seven, is a very effective way to make people feel well disposed toward you.

Listening involves more than your ears. Sometimes just letting a man talk while you listen to him is enough to bring him around to your way of thinking. Walter is a television executive in charge of programming. Roger is in charge of developing projects. Walter has a reputation—well deserved—for turning down new ideas. He prefers to stick to the same old lawyer-doctor-cop shows and family comedies that the network has run for the past decade. Nevertheless, the network is known for its innovative programming. I asked Roger how he got Walter to accept his new ideas. "It's easy," Roger said. "I know Walter is going to say no, but I also know that he is going to tell me at length why he is saying no. And I just sit there and listen. I don't interrupt him. And when he has talked himself out, nine times out of ten he'll say, 'Okay, if you really want to do it, go ahead.' "

This technique works with people who are stubborn, who jump to conclusions, who are opinionated or suspicious. There is no way you can argue them out of their position into seeing things your way or influence them to do what you want. The only way to handle them is to do what Roger did—let them argue *themselves* around to doing what you want. There are three steps to this listening technique:

1. State what you want very clearly.
2. Listen to the other person's arguments. Do not interrupt. Let him talk himself out. If he should pause for a couple of seconds, you can ask him to amplify a certain statement, but do not try to argue with him.
3. When he has finally finished talking—and it may take some time—then react to what he has said by saying, "Yes, I think I understand your point, but I want you to know exactly how I feel about this." And when you finish your brief statement, then let him talk some more. By the time he finishes, he will probably have talked himself out of his original position and adopted yours. If he is still adamant, forget it. You can't win them all.

If you want to flatter someone by letting him know how seriously you are listening to him, use body language to help get the message across. Less than 10 percent of what we communicate to other people is conveyed by words. About 35 percent comes from the way we speak, the tone of voice, whether we mumble or shout; the other 55 percent comes from body movements and facial expressions. So if you are bent on flattering, don't slouch or doodle or write notes to yourself while the other person is talking. Sit up in a relaxed but alert way. Keep your hands still and watch the other person's face. You are telling him more clearly than if you used words that you are listening carefully to what he has to say.

The world's most successful and powerful men have always used flattery to help achieve their purposes. "There is nothing that so kills the ambitions of a man as criticism from his superiors," said the nineteenth-century steel multimillionaire Charles Schwab. "I never criticize anyone. I am anxious to praise, but loath to find fault. If I like anything, I am hearty in my approbation and lavish in my praise."

The opposite side of the flattery coin is criticism. And as Schwab indicated, this will get you nowhere. The average person reacts negatively to criticism. He either becomes angry or is so devastated that he falls apart.

If there is no way to avoid criticizing someone, take pains to make your critique as palatable as possible. Open the conversation, for instance, by reminiscing about a mistake you once made. It is easier for someone to admit that he had been mistaken or negligent if you make it clear that you too have had moments that were less than glorious. Be careful, though—don't give the impression that you are blunder-prone. Don't admit to anything more than the slightest of human errors in your effort to sugar-coat your criticism. Another way is to say, "I may be wrong; I've made mistakes before and I'll probably make them again; but I'm very much concerned about the way you are handling thus-and-so. Let's go over it together and see where we stand." These approaches help the person you are criticizing save face. And by letting him save face, you will make him more willing to do what you want and in the future.

Helping your opponent save face is the key element in any successful negotiation—a labor contract, a lease, getting a bill through Congress, anything. You may be negotiating the price of a house or the terms of a mortgage. Or where to spend your summer vacation. If you want to come out on top and still maintain good relations with the other party—and this is important whether your opponent is the person who will be sharing your vacation or the men who work for you—you must let him or her or them save face. If you are a truly shrewd negotiator, you will manipulate matters so that the other person is grateful to you for being allowed to save face.

Before someone is grateful to you for letting him save face, he must be worried that he will appear as a fool or a failure to the rest of the world if you don't help him. This involves a manipulation within a manipulation.

Suppose the union negotiators are pressing for less work and more pay. Their members are behind them 100 percent. What can you do?

You might point out that if the shorter work week were to go into effect, you would be unable to manufacture enough platinum doorknobs to fulfill your contractual commitments. Therefore you would have to relinquish an important contract. And therefore you would have to cut down on the work force.

Suddenly the union representatives are under attack from the rank and file. "What do they mean," the union members protest, "pushing for a contract that will result in large-scale firings?" The labor negotiators are now on the defensive not only with management but with their own people.

Now you as management can step in and offer a face-saving solution. You offer a slight wage increase and some other concession—perhaps an extra week's vacation after forty-five years of service or a better grade of paper towels in the washrooms—but the work week remains the same. The union negotiators are grateful. They can show their members that they have wrung concessions out of you. They may even be able to convince the rank and file that you wanted to institute a shorter work week for less pay and they fought it like wildcats.

It is not only management that can use the face-saving device in negotiations. Labor can employ it as well—and often does. This outline is a vast simplification of the pattern of negotiations that go on every day of the year. Top negotiators are those men and women who realize that if they do not allow their opponents a face-saving retreat, then the negotiations may string on until neither party has anything to gain or erupt in a mutually destructive strike or bitter confrontations.

The secret is to work out a strategy that will benefit your opponent in some way. But first you have to get your opponent on the defensive any way you can. You have to find some way to get him under attack. This is often done by the offer of a concession linked to an unpalatable demand. He will then be criticized for not grabbing the concession, and his followers will ignore the fact that if he accepted your proposal, they would lose more than they would gain. At this point, he will be grateful for a face-saving out.

REWARDS

Rewards are the pleasantest of psychological tools, but the manipulator should use them sparingly. A reward is just like a good-night kiss. The first one between a young man and woman can be magic, but the minute it is taken for granted, it loses its power to enchant.

The promise of an all-expenses-paid vacation for two at a luxurious resort for the man who sells the most automobiles will get more out of the sales force than any number of pep talks or threats. The executive who tells his assistant that he plans to recommend him for a promotion at the end of the year if he continues his present level of good work is going to get the best work that young man is capable of during that period. The fledgling lawyer who gets an unexpected bonus because of his brilliant research on a complicated case is going to keep on spending long hours of drudgery in the legal library tracking down precedents and rulings.

Rewards can be relatively minor and still be effective. They do not have to be monetary rewards. They can be a handshake and a sincere "Thank you, well done" from the head of the company. Or a warm hug and a kiss when your husband comes home just because you love him and want to show it (and he brought you coffee in bed that morning). The first invitation to the boss's house for dinner is a reward.

Rewards are a form of operant conditioning. A laboratory experiment most clinical-psychology students have to perform illustrates just how this works. A rat is placed in a cage that contains nothing except that rat and a metal bar that protrudes into the cage. The rat, as is the nature of rats, explores the cage thoroughly, sniffing into the corners, stretching as high as it can reach up the walls. At some point, the rat bumps into the metal bar. And when it does, a food pellet comes tumbling into the cage.

Now the rat increases its exploring activity around the area where it found the food. Eventually it hits the bar again and gets more food. It is not long before the rat learns that pushing the bar has something to do with getting food. Eventually it starts pressing the bar in order to get food.

Pressing a bar is not a normal response in animals. Rats in their natural state do not go around pressing metal bars. This is learned behavior.

One can teach humans the same way. And people catch on faster than rats. The lawyer who was given a handsome bonus because of the painstaking research he had done on an important case is encouraged to keep on doing more painstaking research in the hope of another bonus. The husband whose welcome home was especially warm on the day he had brought his wife coffee in bed will be likely to do it more often in hopes of a similar response.

Effective as rewards are as manipulative tools, they should not be allowed to become as routine as the bump-the-bar/get-the-food rat conditioning. The recipient should not learn to count on getting a reward every time. You will get more cooperation and more work out of the individual whose best efforts often go unrewarded.

If you give someone a reward every time he performs well, then he comes to feel that he is owed a reward. And so when you want to motivate that person, you have to escalate the scale of the reward. A weekend for two is no longer enough. It will have to be a week. And a bonus is no longer enough—unless it is accompanied by a raise in salary. You may want to escalate rewards at times—but it should be your decision and not because you have trapped yourself into making rewards seem routine.

Not only do rewards induce people to do what you want because they are grateful and pleased; they can change behavior you do not find helpful into helpful behavior. There is another classic experiment with rats that shows how this works. It illustrates the principle of intermittent reinforcement.

Take the same rat and the same cage. This time the bar mechanism is set up to release a food pellet on every fifth or sixth press, not every time the rat bumps it. The rat does not get discouraged when no food results from bumping the bar. He just continues to bump it— and eventually his bumping behavior is reinforced. He gets a reward. With people this conditioning device works like a charm. Even with very sophisticated souls.

GUILT

"If you want someone to do something for you, make him feel guilty first," a Boston politician said. And he was right. People who have low self-esteem or have suffered a jolt to their self-esteem, such as being put in the position of having done something wrong and feeling guilty, tend to be more willing to put themselves out to do what you want. It offers them a means of expiating their guilt.

An experiment that showed this very clearly was carried out with a group of college students. They were divided into four sections. Each section was told to wait outside a classroom where they would be taking an exam.

The students in the first section waited outside their assigned room until the bell rang. They were then admitted to the classroom and took the test.

While the second section was waiting outside their room, a researcher stopped by and told them that he had just received the results of a personality-inventory test that they had taken earlier. It showed that they were really great guys—self-reliant, self-assured, and responsible.

The researcher then went to where the third section was waiting. He told them that he had received the results of the personality-inventory tests and they had shown that the students were fine fellows. He also told them that he had taken the exam that they were about to take himself and that in each case the correct answer was the second of the multiple choices.

He then told the fourth section that he had taken the exam and that the correct answer was always the second choice. He said nothing about the personality inventory.

After the exam, the director of the study made a point of talking with each student separately. He told each one that he needed help in grading the exams and asked the student if he would be willing to help.

The students in the first section, who had been given no information at all, were unwilling to spend time helping grade exams.

The students in the second section, who had been told the personality inventory showed they were great guys, were not interested either.

Nor were those in the third section, who had been given the answers to the exam, but had also been told that they had great personalities.

But the students in the fourth section, who had been given the answers but not the results of the personality inventory and thus were not thinking of themselves as great guys, were very eager to help out. They felt guilty, and they had no extra boost to their self-esteem to take away the sting of that guilt. Doing something for someone would make them feel better.

Everyone feels guilty at times. Just as everyone feels insecure. And that means that it is relatively easy to manipulate people through guilt. The man or woman driven by an inner need for power will find many variations on the experiment outlined above to make others feel guilty so that they will do what he or she wants.

The idea of manipulating people through their feelings of guilt, however, is quite distasteful, and I do not intend to go into more detail than I have already. It is enough to point out that it is an effective psychological tool.

One should also understand that guilt as a manipulative tool has its limitations. It cannot be employed as consistently as flattery or a calculated system of rewards. You cannot count on guilt. And I will go back to the rats to explain why.

This time we take two rats in two cages. Each rat has learned to press the bar to get food. The first rat—let's call him Clive—presses the bar and instead of food, he receives an electric shock. The second rat—and I'll call him Nigel—presses the bar in his cage. Nothing happens. No food. No shock.

What happens next? Clive stops pressing the bar. That electric shock was unpleasant. Nigel keeps pressing the bar, but nothing happens. Eventually, Nigel presses the bar fewer times, and his bar presses dwindle off to none. There is no reward for the bar-pressing behavior he had learned.

But if you are patient and keep watching, you will see Clive come back and press the bar. If he does not get a shock this time, he will come back and press the bar again and again, even though he gets no food those times either. Eventually Clive gives up too if nothing happens to reward his bar-pressing behavior—or punish it either.

The interesting thing is that if you were to count each bar press, Clive pressed the bar approximately the same number of times that Nigel, who did not receive an electric shock, did.

The lesson here is that while punishment, the electric shock, will suppress a behavior for a while, it does not make that behavior disappear. It is there all the time and will surface when it gets a chance. Even the memory of that electric shock did not stop Clive from pressing the bar. So if you want to manipulate someone, try pleasure tools like flattery and rewards instead of punishment tools like guilt and fear.

And if someone tries to use guilt to manipulate you, let me tell you two things that will make you less vulnerable to this kind of manipulation:

1. Everyone feels guilty at times.
2. The guilts most of us feel are unjustified.

Our guilts stem from insecurity, from expecting too much of ourselves, from a lack of appreciation of our accomplishments and good qualities by bosses, colleagues, friends, and the people we love, which results in lowered self-esteem. You have to remember that they too feel guilty at times—and for the very same reasons. The antidote to your guilt feelings is to tell yourself that you are doing the best you can. That you are a decent person. That you are *not* guilty. And do not let anyone make you believe that you are. If you refuse to feel guilty, the would-be manipulator is powerless.

FEAR

I feel just as strongly about using another person's fear to make him do what you want as I feel about using guilt. Fear is an effective psychological tool in some cases, but it can backfire. The person manipulated by fear carries a potentially explosive load of resentment and anger. He is being coerced into doing something, not doing it because it is what he wants to do—the result that you can obtain through the wise use of flattery or rewards. And as with guilt, fear has its limits. The cornered rat turns on its attacker. So does the man or woman who carries an intolerable burden of fear.

One manipulative use of fear that is less harmful than some depends upon your skill in sizing people up. It works only with people who lack self-confidence.

Take the cases of Marcus and Oliver. You want to sell them something—a fast-food franchise, a block of stock, a corner lot, an encyclopedia, whatever.

Marcus is extroverted and full of self-confidence. To make the sale you stress how he will benefit. He will make a fortune with the franchise. The stock is going to go sky high and he'll make a bundle. In three years' time, he'll be able to unload the corner lot at twice what he paid for it. The encyclopedia will look impressive in his living room and it will be a big help to his kids when they are doing their homework.

If you can convince Marcus that he will profit in some way, you have clinched the sale.

But Oliver is just the opposite. His self-confidence is practically nonexistent. If you want to make the sale, you play on his fears. You use reverse psychology on him. Instead of trying to convince him that he will make a profit, you stress how bad it will be and how much he will regret it if he doesn't buy whatever it is you are selling.

You point out that he is going to feel like an awful fool if he does not buy that fast-food franchise. He is going to see the new owners coining money hand over fist and realize he made the wrong decision. And the same thing with the block of stock. You tell him that no matter what he invests in, nothing else will give him the return that he will get with this stock. If he doesn't buy it, it is just as if he were throwing money away. He owes it to his family to buy the corner lot. Real estate is the only safe investment these days. If the bottom fell out of the stock market, he'd lose everything he had worked to build up, but a corner lot is like owning a gold mine. It is insurance that his wife will never have to go on welfare when he dies. As for that encyclopedia, if he loves his children, he has to buy it. Without an encyclopedia in the house, they won't be able to keep up with their schoolmates whose parents loved them enough to invest in their education.

If you can convince Oliver that he will lose if he does not buy what you have to sell, you have clinched the sale.

The key here, of course, is your ability to size people up. Trying to influence someone without first knowing as much as possible about what makes him tick is like trying to ski blindfolded. A manipulative approach that may work like a charm on someone like Marcus will fail with an Oliver. You do not have to be a psychologist to learn to psych people out. You can teach yourself a lot about how people feel and react.

CHAPTER SEVENTEEN

The Manipulative Handbook

Why Lois could not work with Ben. How to teach yourself why people do what they do. How to change the way people react to you. Writing your own textbook on human nature. What you can see in a woman's eyes. A man's best side—and a woman's.

You have to understand human nature, be a bit of a psychologist, to be an effective manipulator. To get the best result from the four psychological tools—flattery, rewards, guilt, and fear—outlined in the previous chapter, you have to know how people react. Especially how they react to you. Some men and women seem to have instinctive insight into what makes another person tick. Others have to learn it. And it can be learned. What is even better, you can teach yourself.

Lois mastered what she called Human Nature 101, and wrote her own personal textbook to help herself learn what she needed to know. Lois had gone back to work at forty-three when her youngest went off to college. Over the years she had done a great deal of volunteer work—organized the annual antiques show and auction that raised money for the local hospital, run a publicity campaign for the Junior Women's Club, turned her church's Christmas Fair into an event that drew people from neighboring towns, promoted a film festival. When she was ready to go back to work on a regular basis, it was not difficult for her to find a good job in public relations.

But it did not work out the way she had hoped. "I know how to promote anything and everything," Lois said, "but I don't know how to cope with the people in this office. I've never had trouble working with anyone before, but this bunch . . ." and she threw up her hands. "They drag their feet. They're sullen. It's impossible to strike a spark of enthusiasm. I think they hate me."

"Why do you think that?" I asked.

"If I only knew, I'd do something about it," she said.

Just then a young man came into her office. "Here you are," Lois said to him. "I've been waiting for you. I need a dozen of these posters."

"Do you want them that big?" he asked. "If they were smaller, we'd be able to display them better."

"I want them exactly like this one," Lois said in a cold, hard voice. "That's what I said I want. And that's what I want."

"Okay." The young man took the prototype poster off the easel and walked out of the office without another word.

"You see what I mean?" Lois asked indignantly. "They're all like that "

"I see you talking to a nice young man who made what he thought was a helpful suggestion as if he were a schoolboy. You were pretty hard on him."

"I was?" She was astonished. "How? I just told him that I wanted the posters the way I wanted them. The impact they'll make is worth the extra trouble."

"Why didn't you say so?" I asked. "I can't believe

you responded to the volunteers you worked with at the hospital auction or the Christmas Fair that way."

"Well, no," she conceded. "You have to handle those people with kid gloves. If their feelings are hurt or they don't feel fully appreciated, well, forget it. That's the end of their participation."

"Isn't it the same in an office?" I asked.

Lois hesitated. "I suppose so. But after all, they're being paid. They're not volunteers. I don't have to spend time tiptoeing around worrying about their feelings."

"No," I agreed, "but it doesn't mean that you have to go out of your way to *hurt* their feelings."

"You think I did?"

"You certainly did."

"Oh." She was silent.

"Maybe you should start treating your staff as if they were volunteers," I said, "You were always phenomenally successful in getting your volunteers to work like dogs. And love it. You know a lot about human nature. Put it to work."

She laughed. "What I don't know about human nature would fill a book."

And that started me thinking. Maybe what Lois did not know *would* fill a book. I kept turning this over in my mind and came up with the idea for a Human Nature Handbook.

Lois wrote one. And so can you. If you have any doubts about your ability to understand other people, their motivations, their reactions, their hang-ups, then writing your own Human Nature Handbook will help you learn what you need to know.

It is easy enough to do. Buy yourself a notebook, and make daily entries on what you have observed about human nature that day. Or what you have read in newspapers or magazines.

What is the point of writing it down? You learn

more. Before you start writing your own Human Nature Handbook, I suggest you turn back to Chapter Six and review the Five Step Learning Technique. By writing down what you have learned, you are forced to think through the whole episode of the new information. This helps you understand the dynamics of whatever went on, to pinpoint a facet of human nature, and to see how to apply what you have learned to other situations and other people. It also means that you have a record to refer back to. When you have a problem, you can flip through the pages of your own book for help.

"But I can't write a textbook on human nature," Lois argued when I suggested this. "I'm no psychologist. I've had no training."

"I know," I said, "but you'll train yourself by writing. Try it."

And she did. Here is an entry from her book, which deals with the incident that triggered the whole idea.

> February 8. After lunch, I called Ben into my office. "I hear you have a good idea for promoting that series of college rock concerts."
>
> He nodded. Absolutely poker-faced.
>
> I felt like gritting my teeth, but I put on my most sincere expression. I was going to break through to Ben if it killed me. I had promised myself that I was going to counteract the bad impression of the poster episode.
>
> "How about working up your idea so I can present it at conference next week?"
>
> Still a poker face. I got up from my desk, went around and stood beside him, putting my hand on his arm. "Once you have credit for a couple of promotion campaigns," I told him, "you'll be able to do more of the kind of work you like and less of the running-around, errand-boy stuff."

That got him. His eyes opened a bit wider. "That would be great," he said enthusiastically. And I could tell that he really meant it.

"I can give you a rough layout by the end of the week," he said.

I think he's changed his opinion of me.

Lois had gone back to the techniques she had used when she was doing volunteer work, encouraging and praising. She also offered a reward—to show Ben's work at conference. And she had developed insight into Ben's reactions. He had been poker-faced because he suspected that she might take credit for his idea. When it got through to him that she was trying to help him, his whole attitude changed.

That was a very telling observation she made about his eyes' opening wider. Someone once said that the eyes are the windows of the soul. And they may be. Psychologists have discovered that eyes can't lie. If you want to know how a person truly feels about you or an idea or another person or a situation, watch his eyes. The eyes are the source of microexpressions that reveal what people are truly thinking and feeling. Magicians can tell which card in a deck a person is thinking of because the pupils of his eyes will enlarge when that card is exposed. Most men's pupils are larger when they are looking at photographs of beautiful women than when looking at men. If someone agrees with what you are saying, his pupils will expand. If you say something that rubs him the wrong way, they contract.

When a person lies, his eye movements are faster—almost twelve times the usual rate. So if someone suddenly starts blinking a lot when he is talking to you, take this as a warning signal that he may not be telling the truth.

Lois did something else helpful. She got up from behind her desk and stood beside Ben. Everyone has his own space boundaries. Some people react better to a person who is standing close to them; others need more distance. There is even a sex difference in a person's "good side." Lois unknowingly used both these factors in her effort to establish a better relationship with Ben. Ben felt better when he was close to people. He liked it when Lois touched him briefly on the arm. There was no sexual connotation here, simply friendliness.

Most men feel uncomfortable when a woman they do not know well approaches them directly, face to face. They find this alarming. A woman will do better if she approaches a man she does not know or knows only slightly from the side. Women are different. They prefer a face-to-face approach when they do not know the man well.

When I discussed this with Lois, she said, "That's fine for you. You're a psychologist. I thought a lot about this incident when I wrote it down, but I didn't learn all the things you've been telling me from what I wrote."

"Of course not," I said. "But after you have a dozen or so entries like this, you'll be able to draw your own conclusions. That's the way scientists work. They gather information and then they examine it to find the common denominators, to learn what similarities or dissimilarities exist in given situations. That's the way it works."

And that *is* the way it works. Compiling your own Human Nature Handbook will make you more sensitive to people, more understanding. And you will learn an astonishing amount about yourself. The result will be that you will be able to influence people far more effectively—to make them do what you want and to perceive you the way you want them to.

This technique is not valuable only for those people who want power; it will help the man or woman who feels lonely and wants to make friends, who seeks love, or who wants to change the way people think about him or her. When you learn how people react to you and why, you are in a position to change their reactions if you want to. Someone once said knowledge is power. And knowledge of what makes people act and react as they do is an important key to power.

CHAPTER EIGHTEEN

The Marital Checkup

Why you need a checkup. Six key questions and three revealing lists. How to analyze your findings. What anger shows about your marriage. Setting a date for the next checkup.

You are married. And things are okay. You suppose. But not quite the way you thought they would be? Is this all there is to marriage? Where is the secure warmth, the loving tenderness, the delicious fun, the romance that you once enjoyed? That you had expected would last forever? There has been a cooling down. Perhaps a mutual impatience. Disagreements about sex. And money. And you are concerned. Even sad. Because you truly wanted a good marriage. The two of you against the world—as well as part of the world. And the world well lost for love. You are not considering divorce or separation. Yet. But you do sometimes wonder what happened to what you used to have. And wish you could get it back. You can. And it can be even better than it was. This marital checkup will help you get started. It will pinpoint the weak areas in your marriage, so that the two of you can work together to reinforce them.

I advise every couple, no matter how long they have been married, to have an annual marital checkup. It can be the single most important thing you can do for your marriage. And it does not cost a penny. You do not need a marriage counselor or a therapist to guide you. Your own loving common sense and interest in a good marriage are sufficient guide. No stethoscopes or blood-pressure cuffs are necessary. Just two pens and some paper. And an uninterrupted three hours.

This marital checkup will not arouse suspicions, fears, or hostilities. It will evoke pleasant memories and remind you of one shared crisis that you survived. It accents positive areas; encourages a couple to discuss their strengths, to be aware of the rewards in the relationship. It is psychologically designed to help without harming.

MARITAL CHECKUP

Part One

This involves answering six questions and making three lists. They have been designed to clarify your thinking and heighten your awareness of the state of your marriage today.

Here are the questions:

1. What single thing delights me most about my wife/husband?
2. What was the best thing that happened to me in the last twelve months?
3. What was the worst thing that happened to me in the last twelve months?

4. What was the best thing that happened to us as a couple in the last twelve months?
5. What was the worst thing that happened to us as a couple in the last twelve months?
6. If my wife/husband had the power to change one thing about me, what do I think she/he would change?

And here are the lists:

1. Write down ten things you like to do.
2. Write down ten things your husband/wife likes to do.
3. Write down ten things you like to do together.

Part Two

When you finish, exchange your papers and read what your spouse has written; then ask yourself the questions that follow. Allow at least half an hour for this, more if you need it. Do not talk to each other during this part of the checkup. It is a good idea to take this part in separate rooms.

Ask yourself:

1. Am I surprised by anything my wife/husband has written?
2. How do I feel about his/her answer to the first question?
3. How do I feel about his/her answers to questions 2 and 3?
4. Were my answers to questions 4 and 5 the same as hers/his? If not, do I understand why she/he felt that way about those episodes?
5. What about the answer to question 6? Am I surprised? Or does it make me nod and smile? Does

it make me angry? Why? Do I think I can make that change? Will I try?

Now go on to the lists:

1. Did I know she/he liked to do all those things on her/his first list?
2. Was she/he right about what I like to do?
3. How close were our third lists? Do I disagree with anything on her/his list?

Part Three

After you have read your wife's or husband's answers and lists and thought about them, the two of you should discuss what you have found out about yourselves. Are you as close as you thought? Or closer? Or not as close? Are there unsuspected differences in your desires and values? Are there items on your third lists that you have not done together in the last twelve months? This is a good time to make plans to do them in the near future. Your discussion should range freely. Explore all your feelings about these answers and lists.

When you have finished your discussion, there is another topic to discuss. And that is how you feel about each other now. What was the mood of your discussion? Did you laugh fondly at one or some of her/his entries? Did you start reminiscing? Did you say things like "Honestly, I don't know why we haven't gone picnicking (or to the museum, or for a long walk) lately. Let's do it this weekend" or "It's been ages since we had anyone over for dinner and bridge. Let's make a date with the Baxters"? Or did you make plans for even more intimate shared activities?

If you enjoyed the checkup on the whole, if your answers were roughly similar, if your answers to the questions and your lists showed that you were pretty well tuned in to your spouse, if you laughed a little and enjoyed thinking back over the last year, you have a pretty good relationship—sound and healthy. If your goal is a good marriage, you've got one, and awareness engendered by this marital checkup will help you keep it that way.

Or did your discussion turn into a series of complaints? Or regrets that you had done so few things together this past year? Did you get angry?

If you did, this means that the checkup has spotted weak areas in the marriage, just as a physical checkup might reveal that your blood pressure is slightly elevated. The fact that you got angry or complained does not mean that your marriage is on the rocks. It is a healthy sign showing that you care enough to respond honestly to each other. The next step is to discuss just how you think your marriage can be made more satisfying. Make some time tomorrow or the next day when you will have had a chance to do some thinking, to talk about changes. Don't plan anything drastic. Just agree on one area that could stand improvement and work on that. You will find that any improvement in that area radiates out to other areas. In the following chapter, I discuss a psychological tool that you can use to change things for the better.

And now that you have completed this first marital checkup, plan to take it again every single year. It makes the checkup even more meaningful and loving if you schedule it for a day that is important in your lives—the anniversary of the day you met, perhaps, or of your wedding, or of the night you think you conceived your first child: any day that the two of you remember happily. And romantically.

CHAPTER NINETEEN

The Reinforcer

The rat that got shocked. How to turn your strong, silent man into a conversationalist with five cents' worth of sex. How Kathy used positive reinforcement to get her husband to take her out to dinner. How Jonathan used it to get his wife to stay home. How to maintain a constant level of positive reinforcement.

Your marital checkup may have found your marriage in sturdy good health, but it will still need preventive maintenance. A marriage, any marriage, needs constant reinforcement treatment. There are positive and negative reinforcements. Most marriages get too much of the wrong kind. You want to accent the positive.

This is another instance in which we can learn from rats. Remember that experiment in which the rat bumps into a bar that releases a food pellet? And eventually learns that bumping the bar has something to do with getting food? And starts pushing the bar when he is hungry? This is operant conditioning. The rat is conditioned to do what the researcher wants by being rewarded each time he performs the desired act. The reward is a positive reinforcer. The response of the animal produces its own reward.

Now suppose you put another rat in a similar cage. Each time this rat bumps into the bar, he gets an electric shock. It does not take very long for the rat to learn to stay away from the bar. Again the rat is conditioned, but this time by punishment. This is negative reinforcement.

Too many couples use negative reinforcement so skillfully that it makes them miserable. Take the problem of the strong, silent husband. In survey after survey of married women, researchers consistently find that nearly half of them complain that their husbands do not talk to them enough or in any meaningful way. This stems from the way the husbands were brought up. Until just recently, boys were raised to be strong, silent men. This is the male stereotype. And they are just as much victims of it as their wives are. A wise wife can change this state of affairs with just a little effort. All she has to do is make it more rewarding for her husband to talk to her.

The first step is for the woman to stop all negative reinforcement. Do not start telling him everything that went wrong today the minute he comes home from work. Don't whine. Cultivate a pleasant conversational tone. Try to warm up your voice. Make sure that you have something interesting to talk about. It is fine to report on the children, but don't fill your husband in on every little misdemeanor they commit. And don't make him listen to the chronicle of how tired you are, how you could not sleep last night, how bad your cramps are, or how you don't have a thing to wear.

If you discover that this leaves you with nothing to talk about, then start making lists of topics. Read the newspaper so you can discuss the headlines and the sports scores. Bone up on the new-model cars and their relative standings. Are there any new medical breakthroughs in the news that might interest him? What is going on in the neighborhood that concerns you? New zoning regulations, perhaps? Or is your church going to have a strawberry festival this June? You might even discuss the theory of positive reinforcement.

One marriage counselor developed a novel kind of reinforcement therapy for couples when he discovered that most women complained that their husbands did not talk to them enough and most men that their wives would not make love often enough. He instructed each wife to give her husband a penny each time she felt he had made a real effort to talk with her. When the husband had "earned" five cents, his wife "owed" him sex. As the husbands began to talk more freely, the wives felt closer to them, with the result that the quality of their lovemaking improved. And the husbands were so pleased with their wives' increased sexual response that they began to talk even more. The pennies—or really, the approval that they represented—reinforced the desired behavior. They also made it seem like a game, and that helped dissipate the bitterness that had built up when the couples had been using negative reinforcement. The wives, who had felt neglected because their husbands seldom talked to them, had been very stingy with sex. This had made the husbands clam up even more, which had reinforced their wives' sexual coldness.

You don't need to use pennies. A hug or a smile can be positive reinforcement—and even more effective. Positive reinforcement is an attitude as well as an object.

Kathy complained that once they were married, Felix stopped taking her out to dinner.

I could understand why. Felix would call up from the office and say, "How'd you like to go out for dinner tonight?"

"Okay," Kathy would say.

"What do you feel like? Want to go to the Chinese? Or we could try that new Italian restaurant?"

"Oh, I don't care," Kathy invariably responded. "Whatever you feel like."

"Well, what would you like?" Felix would persist. "Maybe we should go back and check out that fish place we used to go to. How would you like that?"

"That would be nice," Kathy would respond. No matter where they went, Kathy never showed enthusiasm over the food or the atmosphere. Her conversation was more or less what it was every night when they had dinner at home at the kitchen table, except when she criticized the service or complained about the position of their table. She had no idea what a turn-off this was to Felix, who wanted not only to please his wife, but also to have a good time.

Eventually Felix got so frustrated that he stopped proposing dinner out. It just did not seem to make any difference to Kathy whether she went out or not. Or where.

It did, of course, but Kathy did not know how to show it. She thought she was being unselfish, letting Felix make the choice. She did not realize that he felt she was not only unresponsive, but unappreciative and reluctant.

"How am I going to switch from negative to positive?" Kathy asked after I had explained to her the effect of her attitude.

"Well, *you* could suggest that the two of you go out for dinner. It's up to you to take the first step. And make sure that you suggest a specific place, somewhere you really want to go. And then make it a pleasant enough evening so that you'll both want to repeat it."

And she did. "I asked Felix if he would take me to a new French restaurant that I'd read about. He said, 'Sure, if you want to go.' So we went. And we both enjoyed it. The food was good, and we liked the way the tables were set with red-and-white-checked tablecloths and bunches of pine needles in pewter mugs. And that gave me my idea. The next Friday night I set the table with the same kind of checked cloth and a little greenery, and I duplicated the menu as close as I could. Felix loved it. He thought my chocolate mousse was even better than what we'd had in the restaurant. We drank a lot of wine, and after dinner we made love and watched television in bed and made love again. And then we went out to the kitchen and finished the chocolate mousse. And Felix said, 'I'd better take you out to dinner more often.' "

Kathy hit the positive-reinforcement jackpot with her first attempt. Now the two of them eat out several times a month. They plan ahead and pick a restaurant that has something special about it. Later, Kathy often tries to duplicate a dish they particularly liked. There has been a double gain. Kathy gets to go out to dinner and she finds cooking more creative and enjoyable.

Withholding sex, withholding smiles, turning sullen, feeling sorry for yourself, whining and nagging—these are negative reinforcements. A positive reinforcement is a reward—and you might review the section on rewards in Chapter Sixteen. If you persevere, you will find that the behavior that made you unhappy is replaced by behavior that you like.

Jonathan used to complain that Sonia was never at home. And he was justified. Monday nights she played canasta. Tuesday nights she went to yoga. Wednesday nights she visited her mother. Thursday nights she stayed home unless there was a movie she wanted to see. And Friday nights she went bowling with the girls. Sonia said, "Well, I'm home Saturday and Sunday nights. We have the whole weekend together. But during the week I'm stuck in the house all day, so I like to get out at night."

Jonathan slowly worked up to feeling very hurt and very angry. His response was to start staying out himself. But what was he to do? He didn't want to go to the movies alone. He did not much enjoy bowling with the fellows. And anyway, most of his friends were married and spent the evenings at home with their wives—just the way Jonathan wanted to. And then he heard about operant conditioning and positive reinforcement.

He realized that there was no point in his not coming home evenings. Sonia was not there to miss him. She would not know whether he was home or not. And besides, this was an attempt at negative reinforcement. The two of them had drifted into this state of affairs. It had not happened overnight, and it could not be changed overnight. The first thing was to make a start. He decided to make that start on a Thursday, the one night when Sonia was likely to be home.

"Let's do something Thursday," he said. "It's been ages since we've gone to a show. How about if I pick up a couple of tickets and we drive in to New York and see a play?"

Sonia was delighted. She met him in the city. They had a couple of drinks, went to the theater, had supper afterward, and drove home happily talking about the play. It was a good evening.

A couple of weeks later, Jonathan said, "I know you've got this standing canasta date on Mondays, but I ran into Sam today and he and Nelly want us to come over next Monday for dinner and bridge. Nelly will call you tomorrow morning. Do you think you could skip canasta this once?"

"I suppose so," his wife said, "and I'd like to see Sam and Nelly. Sure, let's go."

The truth is that Jonathan had not just "run into" Sam. He had telephoned him and made all the arrangements. Jonathan kept coming up with plans every other week or so for things to do together. Sonia was usually willing to cancel one of her standing engagements. Finally one morning at breakfast, Sonia suggested asking Sam and Nelly over for bridge. "We owe them," she said. A few weeks later Sonia said, "You know, we never have a chance to be by ourselves and just talk. I think I might drop out of the bowling team. I haven't been very regular lately and it isn't fair to the others."

Jonathan nodded and said, "I'd sure like it. I agree we never do have enough time for each other."

This was a long-term project, but it was successful. Jonathan realized that boredom had crept into the marriage and a certain indifference, and that this had been reflected in all Sonia's evening commitments. But when he started making an effort to court Sonia again, to make their life more interesting, it worked. Instead of getting angry or trying to lay down the law and tell her she had to be home in the evening (which never would have worked), he used a system of rewards. Whenever Sonia spent the evening with her husband, she discovered that she had a very good time indeed. And that made her want to spend more and more time with him.

Couples whose goal is a good marriage should plan special time together. And regard that time as precious—not to be used to discuss problems or bills, but to catch up on all the things you have been thinking about, that you wanted to tell each other; to spend in long, happy lovemaking, in sitting together holding hands and listening to records, in seeing friends whom you both truly enjoy. Too many husbands and wives with countless demands on their time fall out of the habit of setting time aside for themselves. They end up with ten or fifteen minutes at night before they fall asleep, hardly high-quality time.

If you find that you are little by little cutting down on

that special time you keep for each other or that the quality of the time is degenerating, think about using positive reinforcement. Don't allow yourselves to drift into a Sonia-Jonathan situation. Ask yourself what you can do to make that time more meaningful to the two of you, so that you will look forward to it more, actually be greedy for it.

Sometimes just asking yourself the question is enough. That and telling your spouse that you miss your special times together. Other times you may need to do something to shift your perspective a bit. Some couples find that a second or third or fourth honeymoon helps. Others simply make a point of ensuring that the special time is pleasurable. They treat their spouse as a person who is loved and desired, and she/he responds like a person who is loved and desired.

You can use positive reinforcement to strengthen all the warm and loving and tender aspects of marriage and to suppress the careless, selfish, cold ones. You do not have to engage in a big campaign like Jonathan's—a kiss, a smile, a hug, a homemade pecan pie with whipped cream, a bunch of daisies, a meeting of the eyes are all forms of positive reinforcement. So are the seven magic words of love: "I am so very proud of you."

CHAPTER TWENTY

The Marriage Wreckers

How Elise went wrong. The moving hazard and the long-distance marriage. How children menace marriage. Why you can't count on the halo effect in marriage. Antidotes for the Second Stage Blues.

The only here-today and here-tomorrow person in most of our lives is the one we marry—if we succeed in building a strong enough union to weather the marital hazards. Unfortunately, even the most loving marriages get off course.

Sid and Elise were married in the late 1950s and shared the values and expectations of that decade—a large family and a life of togetherness. Elise found complete fulfillment in her marriage, she reported at her college class's tenth reunion. "Sharing my life with the man I love, giving my children a happy childhood and interpreting the world to them, making a comfortable clean home for them and my husband—these are privileges and joys."

The key phrase in her report was "clean home." The

house was always spotless. The vacuum cleaner was always at the ready. Elise washed and waxed and polished everything that would take a shine. Sid used to swear that she polished the change he left on top of his chest of drawers at night. Elise did not think it was all that funny. She did polish the change. Keeping the house shiny clean came to mean everything to her. The dog was not allowed in the living room. Nor were the children except on special occasions. "They just mess it up," Elise said.

One spring night Sid came home with a fragrant armful of lilacs. Elise looked at them in dismay. "They drip all over the place," she said.

Sid's face fell. "I thought they might remind you of something," he said.

Elise looked at him questioningly.

"It was twelve years ago tonight that we decided to get married," he told her bitterly. "We were sitting on the porch at your folks' house and the lilacs were in bloom. You said that whenever you smelled lilacs they would remind you of that night."

Sid's bitterness stemmed from his memories of the life they had planned together, a loving, family-oriented life with laughing children, close friends, a dog or perhaps two, and an atmosphere of loving, joyous confusion. Not this sterile life in a spotless house with children who never felt free to sprawl on the sofa or play Monopoly on the dining-room table or put model planes together in their bedrooms. Cleanliness had become Elise's most cherished value. She had fallen into the Secondary Gain Trap, very much as Lowell (Chapter Three) had, and substituted a relatively unimportant means for an important end.

On pages 33 and 34 I explained how men and women can avoid such Secondary Gain Traps, and that advice is as valid for marital traps as for any other traps.

Sometimes couples are pushed into a Secondary Gain Trap despite themselves by the hard choices imposed by making a living. For years Americans prided themselves on their willingness to get up and go, to blaze new frontiers; their ability to put down roots again and again. It used to be that families made their own decision to move on. And their motivation was the search for a better life for themselves and their children. But today families are like pawns on a corporate chessboard and are shifted from this corner of the country to that corner according to corporate needs. And what often happens is that the need to earn a living supersedes the family's needs for friends and community and the emotional security that comes from putting down family roots. Psychiatrists and psychologists label one significant segment of their practice "women who have made one move too many." We have learned that while some families survive moves, even seem to thrive on them, other families are destroyed.

Today an increasing number of men are putting their families' needs first. They understand that their wives do not want to live like corporate gypsies. They believe that it is better for their children to continue in school with their friends and grow up to feel that they have a hometown. These men tell the companies they work for, "I'd rather stay in this town at my present level and take my chances on getting a promotion than move to another town and be sure of getting one."

They usually lose their place on the corporate ladder. The man who wants to succeed in business more than anything else in the world does not hesitate when asked to move. He knows that there are always others who would be only too glad to take his place. It is the very rare man who has so much to offer that top management will say, "Okay, he doesn't want to move to Pittsburgh, but we'll move him up anyway."

It will not always be this way. Companies are learning that the man who is willing to say, "My family comes first" is the one who in the long run is going to be the best man for the company. Few men who refuse to move these days will have the bitter experience Charles had eight years ago.

An advertising salesman who worked for one of the big magazines, Charles had moved whenever and wherever the company told him to move—seven times in fifteen years. Then they asked him to move again. The idea of his and his wife's and their five children's and the cat's having to pack up and move again was too much. He said he could not do it. It would not be fair to his family. He was fired. He was told the magazine did not want a man who was not "cooperative."

But companies have discovered that there are a lot of "rebels." And if Charles had made the same decision today, he would probably still be working for the same company. Two years ago a survey of major firms revealed that almost half the employees who had been asked to transfer had refused—ten times as many as had refused the year before. A senior personnel executive, a man who has been responsible for transferring hundreds of employees from city to city, says that his own grown children have turned down promotions because they and their wives want to remain involved in their communities and want their children to have the emotional security of growing up with friends whom they have known since sandbox days.

Agatha told me how she had persuaded Stephen to turn down a promotion that involved moving. "Janie starts second grade next year," she told Stephen, "and she's looking forward to being in Miss Crawford's class.

And I can't bear to leave this house. Look at those dwarf apple trees we planted. They'll bear fruit next summer and we won't be here to eat it. And all those bulbs I just put in. They'll bloom next spring and we won't see them. And the new wallpaper you put up in the bedroom. I can't do it again. I know what it's going to be like. A new house to fix up. Finding a new pediatrician and a dentist and a gynecologist. Having to make new friends again. And never having a husband."

"What do you mean?" Stephen asked.

"You know what I mean. Every time we move, it's months before you surface. You spend all your time at the office or on the road and I feel more like a divorcee than a wife. If you insist on this move, I probably will be a divorcee. Maybe not this time, but next.

"And what about you, Stephen?" she asked. "Do you really want to move?"

Stephen did not want to move. And they did not move.

"We paid a financial price for staying put," Stephen said, "but we had to decide what was more important—my getting another promotion or our marriage. And when you think about it that way, there's no choice. We had always agreed that our marriage was the most important thing in our lives. It was just a matter of taking time to rethink our goals. And marriage was still the most important thing in our life."

There is a brand-new twist to the moving hazard which involves the woman executive. Many women who enjoy their work and are earning good salaries are reluctant to give them up and trail after their husbands to another city where they will have to start at the bottom again.

An even newer twist is when the woman executive is offered a promotion or a position that involves moving to another city. This has given rise to a new phenomenon, the long-distance marriage. It started with couples at the top of the economic totem pole, but is percolating down. *The New York Times* considered the trend to be news worth printing in October 1977.

"John and Adriana Saltonstall are typical of many couples living apart," *The Times* reported, "most of whom are middle-class and upper-class people in their 30's and 40's. Childless and emotionally and financially secure, they decided to separate so that Mrs. Saltonstall, 37 years old, could accept a $37,000 a year job as director of transportation for the State of California. Mr. Saltonstall, a lawyer, remained in Boston. 'We get together every three or four weeks for a long weekend,' Mrs. Saltonstall said. 'We also vacation together.' "

The Times went on to report that several of these marriages had ended in divorce and quoted a marriage counselor who had advised several couples with long-distance marriages as saying, "I think it's crazy. Couples with divergent careers can, with some effort if they consider the relationship important enough, look for ways to deal with both careers."

He may be right or he may not. This is a new and undeniable stress on marriage. There is no right or wrong decision to be made here. All a couple can do is sit down and discuss the situation and decide on what is best for them and their marriage.

This is a time for husband and wife to rethink their goals. What is it they want most in life? Is a good marriage still their goal? Or success in their chosen careers or professions? Does one of them want fame and status more than anything else? This is a time to make use of the Quick List Technique (Chapter Four) to help in establishing or reestablishing priorities.

Goals change. And this is part of life. There is no need to feel guilty. There is a need to talk about your new goals and rearrange your lives in the most loving ways possible so that your new goals can become an integral part of your marriage. You can be successful and have a good marriage. You can be a creative artist and have a good marriage. You can have almost any kind of passionate commitment to knowledge or work in your life and still have a good marriage if you are willing to keep reinforcing that marriage and nourishing it.

The greatest hazard to marriage, however, comes from within. The giant marriage wrecker is the most insidious one. Boredom. Sheer spirit-crushing boredom. Who can say where boredom starts? Or when? But there may come a day when your relationship is suddenly perceived as a ho-hum pairing, brightened only occasionally by a flare-up of sexual passion or a momentary echo of the excitement you used to find in each other. When you are not interested enough to use positive reinforcement or tinker with your halo effect.

One reason I recommend the marital checkup so wholeheartedly is that it gives advance warning of the onset of boredom. The chilling fact is that close to 75 percent of all marriages fall short of their potential because boredom creeps in. This need not happen. Boredom can be kept at bay. Banished. Once you recognize its danger and are aware of its main sources, you can adjust your lives to maintain the necessary stimulation level to keep your marriage vital and lusty. And the earlier the better.

It may come as a shocker, but children sow the first seeds of boredom in most marriages. One of the most depressing studies I have come across is one in which researchers observed some 440 couples going about everyday activities—walking down the street, waiting for the light to change, window-shopping, strolling through the park, pushing a cart through the supermarket. Only six of the couples who had a child or children with them touched each other while they were being watched (and they were not aware they were being observed). And only nineteen of them smiled at each other. The couples without children were much more interested in each other. A third of them held hands, linked arms, or touched in some other way, and more than a third smiled at each other.

In too many marriages children put an end to meaningful communication between husband and wife. Once the children arrive, there is less time for husband and wife to be alone together, less opportunity for intimate conversation, less relaxed, uninhibited time for sex. As the children grow older, they intrude more and more upon parental closeness and privacy. They want to come first. And this is totally natural and hard to resist. But you must. You must put your husband or wife first. Not the children.

Children are owed love and care, total devotion. But they are not owed first place. You and your husband or wife are each other's lover and partner. You created these children. And in much too short a time they will be on their own, making their own homes. And you will be alone together again.

These can be wonderful years that you face if you put each other first; but if you let the children come first, you may discover that the two of you have grown apart, that there is no longer any excitement between you, not even a warm acceptance of each other—just cold boredom. You have not kept your communications open. You turned to your children instead of each other. And now there is an emptiness in your lives.

We tend to think of marriage as a continuum starting with the wedding and proceeding until death or divorce puts an end to it. Actually, marriage is more like a two-stage rocket. It starts off with great fanfare and soars into space until it reaches the second stage, where it sheds first-stage encumbrances and goes on to complete its journey. Many marriages don't make that transition. They succumb to the Second Stage Blues, a particularly corrosive form of boredom. The romantic notion is that the longer a couple are married the more they agree with each other and the better they understand each other. We have discovered that the opposite is the case—the longer a couple are married, the *less* they understand and agree with each other. That old saw about familiarity's breeding contempt is almost true. Familiarity can breed boredom unless one works hard to prevent it.

One of the reasons for this second-stage problem is that in marriage the halo effect tends to become increasingly negative as the years go by—and accents the boring aspects of familiarity instead of its reassuring and cozy aspects. A husband is more liable to see the faults in his own wife than in someone else's wife. And vice versa. After all, he or she has lived with those faults. And because they are annoying, the faults come to assume greater importance than the virtues. Marriage is just about the only relationship in which the halo effect cannot be used consistently to improve one person's view of the other.

Every once in a while, however, the halo effect will turn positive, and this can be a great help in banishing the Second Stage Blues. The way it worked with Patricia and George is a classic example. It was at a New Year's party.

Patricia wore a beautiful floaty chiffon gown, and as she came downstairs she looked smashing. All George said was "Are you ready? We ought to get started." Not a word about how she looked. The truth was that he did not really see her. He saw Patricia, his wife, not Patricia, the beautiful woman.

But Morgan took one look at Patricia when she walked into the party and immediately asked her to dance. "I was going to dance the first one with George," she said hesitantly. "Oh, go ahead," George said. "I want to talk to Vincent."

When George finished his chat with Vincent, he looked around for his wife. She was the center of an animated group. She was sparkling. The rest of the night George watched Patricia. Other men were finding her attractive and amusing. George had lived with Patricia for so long he was surprised that other men were finding her attractive. He did not like the way Patricia looked at breakfast, pale and washed out, her hair in rollers. Her giggle annoyed him. And so did her habits of making clicking noises, of leaving her cigarette burning in the ashtray. And the way she broke into baby talk when they made love drove him up the wall. All these little habits created a negative halo effect which colored George's view of his wife and canceled out his early romantic view of her as beautiful, charming, and witty. But as he watched other men react to her a positive halo effect was created. He began to feel proud of Patricia—and pretty good about himself that he had such an alluring beauty for a wife.

It works the other way too. The woman who has considered her husband pretty much of a bumbler—he can't carve a roast, he's too apologetic when she nags him, he's twenty pounds heavier than when they got married—gets a different view of him one day when she picks him up at his office. There he is behind the desk. And there is his attractive young secretary who obviously thinks he's wonderful. Colleagues come into the office seeking her husband's advice. She discovers that her husband has a whole life of his own where he is a very important person indeed. No bumbler, but an authoritative man in command. That evening her husband may not understand why she makes sexual overtures to him for the first time in weeks or maybe months. His halo effect is very, very positive.

One can use the halo effect consciously (see Chapter Seven), but in the intimate relationship of marriage, with the inevitable irritations that arise—he leaves the toilet seat up, she leaves face powder all over the bathroom basin—you have to engineer positive halo effects very carefully. The negative ones are very strong and always there. It is not easy to ensure that your spouse sees you surrounded by men who find you interesting or as someone who is highly respected by his staff.

It is possible to stage-manage situations that will produce a positive halo effect, but there is always a chance that it might backfire, so be careful. You have to know your husband's or wife's reactions very well. It is quite possible that George might have seen Patricia's social triumph in another way. He could have decided that she was an obvious flirt, chasing after men and making a fool of herself. And the wife who picked up her husband at his office might have zeroed in on her husband's attractive secretary and leaped to the conclusion that he was having an affair with her. It is hard to forecast another person's reactions in cases like this.

The best of these halo-effect bonuses are the product of a kind of serendipity. They just happen. But when they happen—and you'll know when that is—for heaven's sake make the most of them.

You cannot rely on the halo effect to perk up a second-stage marriage, but there are other ways. The most effective antidote for the Second Stage Blues is to develop new mutual interests. Find a new interest, something that is completely foreign to both of you—

and preferably well before the Second Stage Blues set in—that you can work at together.

Several years ago, after Lisa graduated from college, Milt and I bought a dilapidated old farmhouse because we wanted something we could do together on weekends. It was a wreck—unpainted; sagging, leaky roof; rudimentary plumbing; worn linoleum covering heaven knew what kind of floors. Today it is a warm, inviting house. Now we are at work turning a small barn into a guesthouse for when Lisa and her husband come to visit. This whole project has filled our minds and hearts for years now. We talk about it. We discuss living there full time when we are older, what a great delight it will be to watch our grandchildren toddling about. We have planted an orchard and dug flowerbeds and vegetable gardens. Next year our asparagus will be ready to pick. We have developed new skills, new friends; learned about country winters and when to expect the geese to settle on the pond on their way north each spring.

But your antidote to the Second Stage Blues does not have to be a major undertaking. A series of small changes can be enough to keep the zest alive in marriage. Inviting people home for dinner. Getting up early and walking for a mile before breakfast—just the two of you. Buying a sex manual and experimenting with something new. An enterprising and experimental attitude toward sex can do more to counteract the whole gamut of marital hazards than almost anything else. And I discuss ways and means in the following chapter.

If your marriage is endangered by the moving hazard or a Secondary Gain Trap, or the demands of your children and the loss of intimacy, or the Second Stage Blues, or any combination of these stresses, it may be comforting to know that you are not alone. All couples have to deal with some form of marriage-weakening stress. It should be even more comforting to know that there are antidotes for all these. And that there are no right or wrong solutions, but only the solutions that are best for you, for your marriage, for your family. And these solutions, the inevitable compromises, are part of building a good marriage. You build one by living it day by day, year by year, increasing in love and understanding.

CHAPTER TWENTY-ONE

The Key to Great Sex

The one secret of exciting sex. The orgasmic myth. How Julie and Rod turned up their sex thermostat. Writing your own bedroom scenario. How Daisy and Reggie used the Quick List Technique for better sex. How to set up a sex date. The flow peak. Why men fall asleep after making love. Two sex games. The amazing, most common sexual problem today. How to use fantasy and erotica to stimulate desire. Why you should forget about orgasms. The law of reverse effect.

Sex is the vital ingredient in any prescription for keeping marriage vital and loving. It is also an indicator of the state of the union. When sex is disappointing and infrequent, it is usually a sign that other areas in the marriage are cooling down too. You want to keep the thermostat turned up high on sex. It is no place to save energy. When sex is good, everything else tends to fall into place. It is the prime antidote for the boredom that besets marriages from time to time and the best medicine for almost all marital ills, because good sex extends the dimensions of love. And love truly conquers all.

Each couple have to determine their own optimum sexual frequency. Twelve times a week might be right for the Joneses, but the Browns make love once every other week and that is right for them. Most of us fall somewhere between the fever pitch of the Joneses and the controlled passion of the Browns once we have worked out a mutually agreeable frequency. If Tristan wants it every night of the week and Isolde thinks twice a week is too much, there has to be a certain amount of loving negotiation, of mutual give and take. My advice is that Isolde do the giving. She may be sorry if she doesn't. As Tristan gets on in years, if he has not enjoyed a regular and vigorous sex life, his sexual abilities will decline more rapidly than if he had. Isolde can easily turn her "duty" nights into nights of delicious pleasure once she knows—and uses—the single no-fail key to great sex.

The key is, purely and simply—selfishness. That is all there is to it. It is the absolutely correct and natural approach to sex. When you are in the mood for love, you do not say to yourself, "I want to give my lover pleasure." You say, "I want sex. I want to experience those feelings." Selfishness is absolutely justified in sex. It is the most private of pleasures. While your pleasure can enhance that of your partner, she/he cannot feel what you feel and you cannot feel what she/he feels. You experience your own ecstasy.

You must not only be selfish, but take responsibility for your own pleasure. And you must be realistic about what you can expect. Too many people believe the orgasmic myth, with the result that they perpetually feel cheated. They believe that their partner is inadequate and cannot bring them to those peaks which others achieve. Or that there is something wrong with them and their responses.

The truth is that the earth does not move—unless you're bedding down on the San Andreas Fault. The stars do not whirl in the sky. Time does not stand still. But the soul can be shaken. The whole mind-set can be changed. You can be transformed into a mass of feelings and experience a drive to completion that is irresistible. Caught up in sexual flow, you become the creature of your body, pulsing, enjoying, demanding, possessed by a kind of dark heat that propels you to the ecstasy peak. And you fall back into the exquisite relaxation of satiety. This is enough. Truly.

The way to achieve it is by being selfish. This is not an easy rule to follow. Many men and women are so sexually shy and inhibited that they find it impossible to let their partners know what gives them pleasure. Even men and women with considerable sexual experience. Even members of the liberated generation like Julie and Rod.

Julie and Rod never expected to have sex problems in their marriage. Other problems perhaps, but certainly not sex. Julie had lived with a man for a couple of years and had had a number of briefer love affairs. Rod was equally experienced. When they met, "it was dynamite," Julie said. "We took one look at each other and practically fell into bed. It was great. And we discovered we had a lot besides sex in common. After a couple of months, we decided to get married. We were both twenty-eight and we had never had anything like this before. This was it."

"I guess that's where we made our mistake," Rod said. "We never had any problems with sex before we were married."

Rod was wrong. It wasn't marriage, nor was it Julie's decreasing interest in sex. That was only a symptom. Rod now accused her of having faked her sexual interest in him in order to get him to marry her. Julie retorted that the only thing she had ever faked was an orgasm because he was such a rotten lover. Their real problem was that neither of them knew how important it was to be selfish, and both were too inhibited to say what they liked and what gave them the most pleasure in sex.

The first days and nights of sex with a new love are sheer miracles for most couples. There is the excitement of discovery, the breathless passion. It is a glorious time when the hours speed by and the nights are never long enough. But you can't expect it to last. And just as well. There are other things in life that demand your time and energy. That early sexual excitement just has to cool down. But it is not usual for it to cool down as much as Julie's had.

Their lovemaking had become routine. Rod would indicate that he felt like having sex. Julie would agree because she felt she should. But since she was not as eager or as turned on as in the early days of love, she was slow to lubricate, and Rod found entry difficult and she found it uncomfortable. Rod would thrust to climax, all the time resenting Julie's passivity. Julie would often fake an orgasm as a signal to Rod to hurry up and come.

I suggested that Julie needed more arousal time. "Once a pattern of nonenjoyment becomes established," I told her, "it takes time to break it. So it's important that you make sure you have little pleasure successes. Each time you experience sexual pleasure—and I'm not talking about orgasm—you become increasingly greedy for more. A little cuddling and stroking beforehand. A massage. Prolonged kissing. These can make you more receptive—both physically and emotionally."

"I'd like that," Julie said, "but I could never tell Rod to do those things."

"Why not?"

"I'd just be too embarrassed. And then if he did it, I'd be too self-conscious to enjoy it."

"Sex is for pleasure," I pointed out. "There's no reason you shouldn't enjoy it. And Rod will be a better lover if he knows he's pleasing you."

"God knows there's room for improvement," Julie said bitterly.

"How would you like him to improve? What would you like him to do that would make you enjoy sex more?"

"Well, the first thing, I'd like him to do it a lot slower. With Rod, it's 'Come on, let me in, let me in.' And then push, push, push and it's all over."

"But," I reminded her, "you've been faking orgasms so Rod would finish sooner. He's doing what you want."

"I never thought of it that way," Julie said. "But it's not really what I want. That is, I do want to get it over with because I'm not enjoying it. But if it were real sex, I'd want it to go on and on."

"That's what we're trying to get at here. What do you consider real sex?"

"Well, I'd like to have a drink first. And neck a little, so that I feel like I want more. And then when we're in bed, I'd like him to do things a little different sometimes. Like not always being on top. Sometimes I'd like to be up there riding him. Or I like it when we do it sitting up with out legs wrapped around each other. Nothing kinky—I don't like that—but just something different. And oral sex. I love to be licked, but Rod never does anything like that."

I listened quietly as Julie talked about her sexual desires, and when Julie stopped, I asked, "What does Rod say when you ask him to do these things?"

Julie looked shocked. "I told you. I could never ask him. I'd be too embarrassed. Anyway, he's a man. He should know. He's had plenty of experience."

"He may be experienced, but he's not a mind reader. You have to tell him what gets you excited, what gives you pleasure."

Later that day, I had a similar conversation with Rod. "If Julie would just act the least bit romantic," he said, "I'd appreciate it. But she just gets into bed, spreads her legs, and lies there like some long-suffering martyr. I always come, but it doesn't make me feel all that good. She makes me feel as if I'm raping her sometimes. And I keep thinking about how it used to be. She used to be so responsive."

"If you could write the scenario," I asked him, "how would it go?"

Rod smiled. "God, if I could write the scenario! Well, I'd like it if I came home from work and Julie was there already. Nowadays it seems to me she stays at work later and later. And there'd be candlelight. And a bottle of white wine in a cooler. And Julie'd be wearing something pretty—not the jeans she always gets into when she comes home. I gave her a fantastic negligee for her birthday—all lace, you know. And . . ." He waved his hand in a curve. "And we'd have a glass of wine." He stopped, obviously embarrassed. "It's so adolescent."

"Nothing is adolescent," I said. "What happens next?"

"Julie would have put on one of my old big-band tapes. And I'd say, 'Let's dance.' And we'd swoop around to the music. A tango, maybe. And then I'd dance her right into bed. And she'd undress me, and— well, that's about it. We'd make love. And then we'd have some wine and something to eat and make love again, and this time she'd suck me."

"Have you suggested this to Julie?" I asked.

"She'd think I was crazy," he exclaimed. "Off my rocker. She'd either laugh at me or get mad and say something sarcastic about being sorry she wasn't romantic enough for me anymore without putting on an act."

Both Rod and Julie considered themselves sexually sophisticated, but they were too inhibited to tell each other what gave them pleasure—even when it was obvious that their sex relationship had turned from sweet to sour. But they wanted to do something about it. They wanted to get back the excitement they used to have.

This was not a serious case of sexual malfunction or dysfunction, and the cure was relatively simple.

I asked them individually to write down the sexual scenarios they had outlined—and when they had done this I asked them to exchange the scenarios. They were shocked to discover how much alike their scenarios were. There was nothing that turned them off or disturbed them in each other's sexual desires. They found it a little embarrassing to discuss the scenarios at first, but once they got started it was as if a dam had broken. Their inhibitions were being swept away in the first real discussion they had ever had about sex.

There was one more step for them to take. "I don't want you to have sex until Saturday night," I said. "That's five days from now. Make a sex date for Saturday night and play out your scenarios. Be thinking of them during the week. And then on Saturday, raise the curtain on a new and better love life." My reason for telling them not to have sex for five days was to raise their anticipation level, make it a very special occasion.

They followed instructions. And they liked the result. Their sex life has improved greatly. Julie doesn't fake orgasms anymore. She doesn't have to. Julie and Rod learned that selfishness pays off in sexual pleasure and that since neither one of them is a mind reader, it is up to them individually to take the responsibility for their own pleasure by indicating clearly what pleases them most.

The sex date is a tremendously effective way to restore excitement to your sexual life. Sex can be bread-and-butter sex or caviar-and-champagne sex. You need both kinds. Bread and butter is the day in, day out, comfortable sex that binds a couple together. Caviar-and-champagne sex is anticipated sex, when there is plenty of time and no pressures. This is the kind of sex you make dates for. And if you find it difficult to discuss your sexual desires with your partner, there is nothing wrong and everything right with your writing your own sex scenarios and exchanging them a few days before your sex date, the way Julie and Rod did. Even couples who have been together for decades will discover fresh pleasures or rediscover forgotten delights this way.

Daisy and Reggie had three teen-aged children. "So you know for sure we've done it three times," Daisy said. Their sex life would have made those hypothetical Browns who make love once every other week seem sex-crazed. Daisy and Reggie averaged once a month. And as Reggie said, "It wasn't anything to write home about."

This cooling down was no sudden development. But recently a number of other things had started going wrong with their marriage. All the irritations and petty annoyances that are part and parcel of any intimate relationship had suddenly escalated into major issues. Both Daisy and Reggie were sophisticated enough to feel that if they were able to improve their sexual relationship other aspects of their life would also improve.

In many ways theirs was a more difficult problem than Rod and Julie's; it had gone on longer, and Daisy and Reggie were even more inhibited about discussing sex. There was no question of asking them to write love-making scenarios. Reggie would have said that it was nonsense and refused to put anything down on paper. Daisy would have been equally unwilling to reveal her inner desires.

I explained the Quick List Technique without telling them what I would ask them to list, simply saying it was a way of identifying goals. They agreed to try it. Then and there. I gave them each paper and pencil. "When I say 'Go,' I want you to write down, just as fast as you can, the three sexual acts you like most. Don't stop to think. Just write what comes into your head first. You have thirty seconds. Go!" And they scribbled away like industrious schoolchildren.

At the end of thirty seconds, I said 'Stop!' and picked up their papers. Daisy's list read:

1. Finger fucking
2. Cunnilingus
3. Tongue kissing

Reggie's list was:

1. Being sucked
2. Being sucked
3. Being sucked

I suggested that they both try being selfish and making sure that they got what they wanted when making love by telling each other just exactly what they wanted. I also asked them to keep a sex diary for the next two weeks—noting when they made love.

Two weeks later they returned. Reggie handed me their sex diary. Monday—no sex. Daisy had stayed up until midnight baking cookies for the monthly PTA lunch. Tuesday—no sex. Reggie had to work on his income-tax return. Wednesday—sex. But just when it got interesting, one of the kids had a stomach virus and began vomiting, so Daisy had to go hold his head and get him settled comfortably back in bed. Thursday—no sex. Neither of them felt like it. Friday—sex. "I didn't come—as usual," Daisy reported, "but I liked it. I really got interested." Saturday—no sex. Their daughter had three girls over for a slumber party, and Reggie and Daisy didn't feel comfortable—even with the door locked. So they went to sleep instead. And so it went.

"This is encouraging," I said.

"You think so?" Daisy exclaimed, unbelieving.

"Absolutely. This shows that you made love three

times in the past two weeks, as often as you made it in the last three months. And even if Daisy didn't have an orgasm, she enjoyed lovemaking. This is real progress."

"Perhaps," Reggie said. "At any rate, I've come to realize how we got into this fix—or part of the reason. With three kids in the house, it's impossible to make love without worrying about whether one of them is going to start knocking on the bedroom door."

"You can solve that problem if you try," I said. "The important thing is that now that you're beginning to learn that selfishness pays off in sex, you're ready to revolutionize your sex life. I want you to make a sex date once a week for the next month. Make time for yourselves. Send the kids to a movie on Saturday night. Or to the high school basketball game. If there's no way to get them out of the house so you can be alone together and feel free, then think about checking into a motel for a few hours. Put your minds to working out a way to have a few hours every week that belong to you and you alone. Hours to be devoted to sex.

"These are precious hours, so you should plan just what you want to do in this time."

"Well, it's obvious what we're going to be doing," Reggie said.

"Yes, it is," I agreed, "but there's more to it than that." I explained that I think of lovemaking—the caviar-and-champagne kind of sex—in terms of a party. There is the planning and preparation—putting clean sheets on the bed, making sure that there is something good to eat and perhaps a bottle of wine (watch the drinking however; just one sip too many may spoil the party. Alcohol is a depressant and can depress a penis as well as a mood), burning incense or perfumed candles in the bedroom, arranging for the children to have a sleep-over date at a friend's house (and you, of course, will return the favor), deciding what to wear (and it is as important for a man to have a handsome dressing gown as for a woman to have a lacy seductive little something). Then there is anticipation, when you think about what you will be doing and when you sip your wine, flirt by candlelight or firelight. All this helps turn you on and get you into the mood. And then there is the party itself. The lovemaking should be as prolonged and imaginative and delightful as you can make or want it.

The best sex comes when you achieve a state of flow (see pages 74 through 78 for an explanation of flow). This is when you are totally absorbed; when you do not think about what you are doing, but instinctively progress from one pleasure level to the next until you peak. You cannot expect to experience sex flow every time you make love, nor should you want to. Comfortable bread-and-butter sex, what one man calls "sleeping-pill sex," that warm reaffirmation of closeness and attraction, is important. The peak experience loses its impact if it becomes the norm. And it can become emotionally exhausting if you strive for it every time, whereas the cozy, go-to-sleep kind of sex is an emotional restorative. The two work together, and the wise couple will enjoy this balance of nature and not try to change it. Afterward there is pillow talk—affectionate confidences, relaxed love talk. There is a very special emotional intimacy that follows sexual intimacy. Too many men miss this by rolling over and falling asleep after sex. Scientists have only recently discovered that the reason so many men do this is that their climax seems to provoke a neurologic response in the brain that triggers a momentary sleepy feeling. If a man will decide that he is not going to let himself fall asleep, he will discover that in a minute or two he no longer feels sleepy. And he will not have cheated himself of the tender intimacy of pillow talk, which is as much a part of the complete sex act as the caress or penetration or orgasm.

Both Reggie and Daisy nodded. "I see what you

mean," Daisy said. "Really think of it as a date, the way we used to sixteen years ago."

"That's right." And since they were so much more relaxed now, I told them about scenario therapy and how it had helped Julie and Rod and other couples; how the scenarios spur lovers on to inventive and delightful peaks in their efforts to make their sex dates true champagne-and-caviar occasions.

One woman told me she had invented a sex game that she and her husband now played every Sunday afternoon. A pair of dice is all that is required. They throw the dice three times. The winner then orders the loser to do whatever he or she wants. It takes quite a while to get to the actual sex act, because they start their play fully dressed in the living room. The first few rounds are devoted to getting each other undressed and into the bedroom. There are times when one partner wants to make love on the living-room floor in front of the fire and the other wants to be in bed. It can take some time before such issues are resolved.

"We do silly things," the wife confided, "like ordering each other to do sex exercises or to masturbate or to try some gadget that we've seen in a magazine and sent away for. We have a whole locked closet of sex toys. I always have something good to eat prepared beforehand. A cold roast chicken. Or a casserole that I leave warming. And we do have champagne and caviar sometimes. Our sex dates usually last well into the night."

Another couple have their own Monopoly game which they keep locked away from the children and play behind locked doors. They have marked up the title-deed cards so that each has a double price. The rent on St. Charles Place, for instance, is $10 plus a kiss, while the rent on Connecticut Avenue with three houses is $300 plus the tenant's stripping to the rhythm of a belly-dance record, and the rent on the Boardwalk with one hotel is intercourse in the owner's preferred position. While one partner may prefer certain activities to others, the rule of the game is that nothing can be penciled in on the cards that is offensive to either one.

When I told one lecture audience about sex dates and sex scenarios and sex games, a woman came up to me afterward and asked, "What's the point of something silly like that? I can't imagine me and my husband or any of the husbands and wives I know getting involved in that kind of nonsense."

"You'd be very much surprised at the kinds of 'nonsense' even the most seemingly staid couples enjoy," I said. "And this 'nonsense' is important. Sex researchers have discovered that the greatest sex problem that exists today is—unbelievable as it seems—lack of desire. Specialists report that the single sex problem both men and women consult them about most frequently is lack of desire. These husbands and wives are concerned enough to consult their doctors. And they're right to be concerned."

There are many reasons for lack of desire. Sometimes it is the woman who keeps demanding more and more. Her husband finds himself unable to meet her sexual demands, with the result that in a very short time his desire has fled. Sometimes it is the woman whose husband consistently fails to bring her to orgasm who discovers that her desire has diminished to the vanishing point. But most often the culprit—or the criminal—is boredom. Boredom and sex are just like oil and water; they don't mix.

So if a sex scenario or a sex date or a sex game can keep sexual excitement alive, I am all for them and any other effective techniques for sparking desire and keeping sex exciting.

Two of the most effective sexual turn-ons and desire initiators are fantasy and erotica. Some people tend to feel guilty or embarrassed about using them. There is nothing wrong with fantasizing about having sex with another lover or lovers in another place before sex, during sex, even after sex (when it may help spur you on to another round). Almost everyone does it. If a woman gets pleasure by fantasizing that she is making love in front of a formally dressed male audience or with five men at the same time or that she has been tied with silken cords spread-eagled on a four-poster while a masked man ravishes her, that is fine. Dream about your secret scenarios until you begin to respond sexually. And if your mate is not available, then go ahead and masturbate. Be selfish. Give yourself the pleasure you want. You will find that by using your favorite daydream or combination of daydreams you will soon begin to lubricate almost instantaneously. A man's fantasies often have to do with making love with two women or watching two women make love or having a woman dressed in black net stockings and a garter belt order him to satisfy her. Anything goes in a fantasy. The point of the exercise is pleasure. Your pleasure.

As for erotica, you might call it pornography, although I myself happen to find the word "pornography" a turn-off and "erotica" a turn-on. Both men and women are stimulated by watching erotic films, looking at erotic paintings or photographs, and reading erotic novels. One middle-aged couple who had not made love in months went on an erotic-movie binge when they visited New York and saw three films, one right after another. "By the third film," the wife reported, "we were sitting there in the dark caressing each other, getting all hot and bothered and acting as if we were teen-agers. Sam found a place where you can rent sex films, and we're going to try that when we get home."

It used to be thought that women did not respond to pornography, but they do—every bit as much as men. In one revealing experiment, couples were shown an explicit film in which a man and woman made love in several extraordinary positions. Half of the audience was told that the couple in the film were newly married; the others were told that the woman was a prostitute and the man her client. Without exception, the viewers reported that they felt excited while watching the film. There was absolutely no difference between the men and the women or between those who had been told that the couple were married and those who thought they were watching love for pay. The only significant difference was that more women than men thought the couple were having a good time.

After lack of desire, the most prevalent sex problems seem to be premature ejaculation and inability to get or maintain an erection for men and inability to achieve orgasm for women.

Duncan and Peg were characteristic of many couples. They allowed their sex life to cool down so drastically after the children were born that when they wanted to resurrect it, there was no spark left in the ashes. Duncan could not get it up and Peg could not come.

They had not realized how dismal a state they had reached until they went on a second honeymoon when the twins were eight. Ever since the twins had come home from the hospital, Duncan and Peg's sex life had turned into a sometime thing. Peg was perpetually exhausted when the twins were infants and even more exhausted when they began to walk. Duncan accepted this, and while he would have liked a more active sex life, he understood why Peg fell into bed every night like a log. What he did not understand was that it would have been well worthwhile to spend some money now and then on sitters so that he and his wife could have time to themselves. This was a classic case of parents' putting their children first instead of each other.

But they had high hopes of their second honeymoon

and were looking forward to those ten days. But right from the beginning, it was a disappointment. Peg felt fat and unfashionable when she looked at the other women—many of them on their first honeymoons—at the resort they had chosen. And Duncan felt tired and bald and old. Peg had bought a new bathrobe, but its matronly practicality made her regret that she had not splurged on something more feminine and alluring to wear when they had breakfast on their terrace overlooking the ocean. And Duncan found himself comparing Peg with the slim young brides riding bikes and gazing adoringly at their new husbands. He privately thought he would have had a better time if the twins had come along.

It was not until the third night of the vacation, however, that despair set in. It was also the third night that Duncan had been unable to get an erection. And when he tried to bring Peg to orgasm by masturbation, she could not come. He felt inadequate and guilty. Peg felt unattractive and inadequate. By mutual—although silent—consent, they did not attempt sex during the rest of this second honeymoon.

My suggestion was that, for the time being at least, they stop worrying about it. "Forget about erections and orgasms. Both of you."

"That doesn't leave much," Duncan objected.

"It leaves plenty. A whole world of pleasure that you haven't tasted for years," I said. "The two of you are so busy being guilty and feeling inadequate that you aren't allowing yourselves to find any enjoyment at all in sex. Guilt ruins your self-esteem, and that makes your sexual pleasure slide down to the vanishing point. It's been called the law of reverse effect. The harder you try to perform, the less well you perform and the less pleasure you have. And pleasure is what matters. Not erections. Not orgasms. Stop thinking about sex as a performance.

You don't have to perform. Concentrate on selfishly obtaining as much pleasure as you can."

"But that's not sex," Peg said. "It's just—why, it's just fooling around!"

"Fooling around is more important than you think. Try it."

The secret of better sex for couples like Duncan and Peg is usually learning to relax by concentrating on pleasures that can be enjoyed in a leisurely exploratory way with absolutely no pressure to bring the other to a climax. I recommended that they do all the things they probably had not done since their courting days. To caress each other slowly. To kiss and kiss again. To lie close to each other and talk. To shower or bathe together. I also suggested they buy a couple of sex manuals. The majority of these are written by responsible men and women, most of them physicians or psychologists, and very helpful. To get the most out of such a manual a couple should read it together—preferably in bed—in a relaxed frame of mind. "Be ready to laugh at some of the advice and the positions," I told them. "Don't take it too seriously. And don't feel you have to work through all seven hundred and six positions a book might advocate. If you discover two or three that appeal to you or find something that turns you on, you've more than gotten your money's worth. Some of these books also suggest exercises to increase your sex potential. Those are fun to do together.

"The most important thing," I stressed, "is to get back into the sex habit. Forget about performance and concentrate on all the selfish pleasures you can enjoy together."

It was six weeks before I saw them again. And they were transformed. Peg had lost at least ten pounds and looked years younger. Duncan had also lost weight and carried himself more confidently.

"Something must be agreeing with the two of you," I said.

"Sex," said Peg. Their sex life had truly improved. Duncan had found that when he stopped feeling inadequate he often surprised himself. And Peg had discovered that when she didn't strain for orgasm but concentrated instead on enjoying the sensations of the moment, lovemaking was far more gratifying. Now that the emphasis had shifted from performance to pleasure, they had discovered a world of far greater sexual fulfillment.

And this had triggered another change in their lives. "We really took a look at ourselves," Peg said, "and decided we had let ourselves go terribly. I kept remembering how dowdy and fat I felt on our second honeymoon and how jealous I was of all those slim, attractive young women. And I'm not even forty yet. So we both agreed to diet and exercise. We go bicycling together every night before supper. The twins go with us, so it's really a family affair and a lot of fun. And the boys are very proud of their dad now that he has lost that paunch he'd developed. You'd be surprised how many ways sex is making our lives better."

The same prescription of emphasizing pleasure instead of performance also applies to the problem of premature ejaculation. Too many men worry too much about this, with the result that it diminishes their sexual pleasure. Many men, especially early in their sex lives, find it difficult to delay ejaculation. All they can think about during lovemaking is their climax—and how to postpone it. Some men do the nine-times table in their heads or recite the alphabet backward to themselves to keep their minds off what they are doing. This can make for terrible sex.

It is up to the woman to assure her partner that she is

not going to think he is a lousy lover if he reaches climax immediately—or before she does. For most men, this lifting of the performance pressure usually results in a longer time before ejaculation. But even if it doesn't, lovers should keep in mind that many, many women find it difficult if not impossible to reach orgasm with the normal thrusting of the penis in the vagina—and reach absolutely staggering orgasms when their lover masturbates them after he has climaxed. So I suggest that men stop worrying, let themselves be selfish, and go ahead and enjoy, with the knowledge that there is more than one way to bring a woman to orgasm. Sex should never be allowed to degenerate into a trial by performance for either partner.

The keys to exciting sex in this chapter, from being selfish to making sex dates to using fantasy and erotica as turn-ons to thinking pleasure, not performance, are all variations of two important psychological tools. One is the same kind of Pavlovian advice that is part of the learning techniques outlined in Chapter Six. You can condition yourself to experience desire in much the same way that Pavlov conditioned his dogs to salivate. It is a matter of associating certain fantasies or settings or song lyrics or acts with sexual pleasure. The more you do it, the faster your response will become to these stimuli. The woman who once needed a long arousal time will find herself in a sexy mood much faster once she has conditioned her mind to turn on her body when a certain song is played, when she reads a sexy novel, or when the nape of her neck is licked or whatever.

The other psychological tool is that old faithful—and reliable—the reward. The more pleasure you derive from sex, the more sex you want. This also relates to the rule for succeeding in business that instructs you to arrange your life so that you experience a certain amount of success every day or every week. You should structure your love life so that you will have some sexual pleasure every day or week.

By now, these techniques should be very familiar to you—so familiar that you can use them to develop your own, very personal ways to make your sex life even more exciting. Think positive reinforcement. Think pleasure, not pressure. Sex can be a delightful and integral part of your marriage and give your lives together the kind of lusty delight that makes life worth living. It can add to and strengthen love, which is everyone's ultimate goal.

CHAPTER TWENTY-TWO

What Is This Thing Called Love?

The elusive emotion. How to tell what your own love needs are.

I have left the best until last. Love. To love and be loved is the ultimate goal, the most blissful state of existence imaginable. But what is love? Poets write about it. Singers sing about it. Scientists carry on solemn debates about it. Sigmund Freud himself admitted, "We really know very little about love," and up to the end of his life this man who turned sex into a subject for dinner conversation refused to even try to define love. "I have not found the courage to make any broad statements on the essence of love," he said. "Our knowledge is not sufficient."

About the best definition, I feel, is "caring as much about the aims and well-being of another person as you care about your own aims and well-being"; and I have always relished the homely reality of poet and essayist Judith Viorst's definition of love: "When you're in bed and he's half-asleep and you can't sleep because you've got to have a glass of cold water and he climbs out of bed and gets you the water." That *is* love. Even when he grumbles.

Someday, perhaps, we will be able to define this elusive emotion more precisely. But a U.S. Senator made headlines not too long ago when he scornfully questioned the use of taxpayers' money to fund a study to find out more about love. Love is not a serious subject, it would seem. Not worthy of study. Not practical. Not useful. Yet love is what most of us want more than anything else in the world. Other goals—money or success or power, for instance—are often love substitutes.

While we may not know just what love is, we do have more insight into the psychological triggers and components of love than we used to. Some of these new findings contradict long-cherished beliefs about love. Since I believe that the more one knows about love the easier it is to go about putting more love into one's life, I have developed a quiz based on the new research to help people distinguish love facts from love fiction. This abbreviated version will allow you to rate yourself on your love knowledge. Respond to each statement with Fact or Fiction. The correct answers and explanations for the answers are at the end of this chapter.

FACT OR FICTION LOVE QUIZ

1. A man or woman will experience only one true love in life.
2. When you are deeply and truly in love, it absorbs all your energies and thoughts.
3. If someone loves you, he or she will never exploit you.
4. Women's love needs are different from men's.

5. Men have a greater capacity for true love than women.
6. Everyone has the ability to fall in love.
7. Hate is the opposite of love.
8. Most people fall in love with someone who reminds them of their parent of the opposite sex.
9. Men are more interested in sex than in love.
10. When you are in love, you understand the person you love completely.
11. Men handle serious love problems better than women do.
12. If you will just wait, you are bound to find the partner of your dreams.

Now that you have checked your answers, have any of your previous convictions or theories of love been exploded? If you had ten or more correct answers, you know just about as much about this thing called love as most researchers do. But how much do you know about your own love needs? Do you know what qualities a man or woman must have to stir your love? With most of us, this knowledge is buried beneath the conscious reasoning level. By bringing it to the surface, you may be able to fill those needs faster and better. There is a simple diagnostic test that will probably tell you more about the qualities you seek in the opposite sex than you have been aware of. It is a variation on the Quick List Technique that is extremely effective in pinpointing a person's love requirements.

FINDING OUT ABOUT YOUR OWN LOVE NEEDS

You will need five sheets of paper.

1. On the first sheet, write down the first ten things that come into your mind to describe yourself.

Don't sit and ponder over them. Just write down ten qualities or characteristics as fast as you can. It should take less than a minute.

2. Now, think of the first meaningful romance you had. It may have been puppy love. You may have been ten or eighteen or twenty-five. It does not matter. All that matters is that it is the first strong romantic relationship in your life. Now write down the first ten things that come into your mind describing that person.

3. Think of someone of the opposite sex who is or was a very good friend of yours, someone you were very fond of, but never thought of in a romantic way. It may have been the boy or girl next door when you were going to school. Or someone you met when you started work. But it was always a platonic friendship. On the third piece of paper, write down the first ten things that come into your head describing that person.

4. On the last sheet of paper write down the first ten things you think of that describe the person you are now married to or in love with. If you are not in love with or married to anyone, describe a person of the opposite sex to whom you are strongly attracted. And if there is no one, then you do not have to make this fourth list.

When you have completed the lists, spread the four pieces of paper in front of you. Many of the characteristics will appear on all four lists. Look for the qualities that your first romantic love and your present love possess that you and your platonic friend of the opposite sex do not possess. Write those qualities down on the fifth piece of paper. These are the qualities that have drawn you and your present love together. If you were to fall in love again, your new love would undoubtedly possess some or all of these qualities. These are qualities that you see as complementing you, making you a more whole person. They are also the qualities that will probably cause the most trouble in your love relationship, because they are strange to you. You do not possess them. They have a kind of hidden electric charge that is both positive and negative, that can attract and repel. But these are qualities that you want in the person you love.

Now if you did not make the fourth list because there is no loved person or potential love in your life, you still have a fair indication of your love needs by isolating those qualities your first love possessed that you and your platonic friend do not. And when you do meet someone who attracts you, try making the fourth list then. You will probably detect several resemblances to your first romantic attachment.

One of the facts that we have established about love is that it fills a need. It offers positive reinforcement. It is rewarding. In the next chapter, I outline some of the new findings on the first stage of love—attraction—and how to use what you have learned about your love needs to attract people to you.

LOVE FACTS AND FICTIONS

Here are the answers to the love quiz on pages 220-221.

1. FICTION. If a man or woman is capable of loving another person, he or she has the capacity to love many times and many people. This is why widows and widowers can have happy marriages. And there are many kinds of love. Parents love all their children, not just one.

2. FICTION. Love acts to expand your capacities and increase your drive and energy. It stimulates

the imagination and makes people more eager to achieve.

3. FICTION. Love often involves exploitation. A man may love a woman and yet take advantage of her love for him to ask that she put his interests first and subordinate her desires or career to his.

4. FICTION. Both men and women need to be desired, admired, and assured of the other's love.

5. FICTION. Studies show that women have an infinitely greater capacity for love than men.

6. FICTION. Some people cannot love. Some have deep-seated emotional blocks that do not permit them to love. Others are too self-centered to give love.

7. FICTION. If there is an opposite to love, the closest thing would be indifference. The fact is that love and hate are very closely related. It is quite normal for people to have occasional flashes of hatred for the person they love.

8. FICTION. We used to believe this, but research has demonstrated that both men and women tend to seek a mate who has the best qualities of their mother.

9. FICTION. A recent survey of more than four thousand men found that more than a third of them believed that love was the most important thing in life and another third were convinced that love made sex better.

10. FICTION. The more deeply in love you are, the worse your judgment is about the character and temperament of the person you love. The old saying that "love is blind" has a lot of truth in it.

11. FICTION. Women seem to cope better with disappointment in love than men. Three times as

many men as women commit suicide because of unhappy love affairs.

12. FICTION. Very few men and women ever find the partner of their dreams. The person we fall in love with is usually completely different from our picture of the ideal husband or wife.

CHAPTER TWENTY-THREE

Love Lines

Where to find your true love. How to tell whether it is love or infatuation. Establishing a line of social credit. Believing in your own lovability. How to attract another person. When to use selective reticence. The tattletale eye of love. Why you should check the moon when making dates. The ultimate goal.

It is one thing to be aware of your own particular love needs. It is another to find love. The man or woman who seeks love must first be visible. The man who spends all his spare time watching television, the woman who rarely leaves the house, the office workers who hold themselves aloof and scurry home to lonely evenings, people who do not involve themselves with others seldom find love (and research also shows us that they die at a younger age than those men and women who are more extroverted). One rarely trips over a prospective wife or husband between the television set and the refrigerator. You have to let the world know that you exist and show people that you are interested in them. Finding love is like catching fish: you have to have your lines out.

One would think that this would be second nature,

but to judge from the hundreds and hundreds of letters I get every year asking how to meet people, it obviously does not come naturally to many men and women.

It truly is not so difficult to find someone to love and to love you. One of the things statisticians have discovered is that most people marry someone who lives in the same town and usually in the same neighborhood. More than half the people who got married in one three-month period in Columbus, Ohio, for instance, married someone who lived no farther than sixteen blocks away. Other studies have shown that the majority of married couples lived within walking distance of each other before marriage.

You may even know the person you will eventually fall in love with and marry this very moment. Most people fall in love with someone they already know—someone at the office, in the neighborhood, someone they went to school with, someone they play bridge or Mah-Jongg or tennis with. You may not even suspect that you love him or her yet.

The first stage of love is attraction—when someone is drawn to you, singles you out as being particularly interesting or amusing or downright adorable. It can be instantaneous, that magic meeting of the eyes "some enchanted evening across a crowded room." But more often the initial attraction is simply a heightened interest that increases bit by bit until each is aware that the other has become a very important person in his or her life. Can this be love? Who knows? It may be no more than a passing attraction. It may be infatuation. Or it may be love.

Attraction between a man and a woman is largely sexual. They may have friends and interests in common, but it is sex that ignites the spark. The attraction may flare up and then disappear in a matter of days, or it may be so strong that the couple are absolutely smitten with each other. This is the infatuation stage. If it is no more than infatuation, it will run its course in six to eight weeks. Often less. One person may remain strongly attracted for days or even weeks after the other has cooled off, but two months is usually the outside limit of the intense mutual attraction we call infatuation.

Love is different. It lasts and grows stronger day by day. As the relationship progresses, the couple become more emotionally, intellectually, and physically involved. They often perceive each other differently from the way they did in their initial encounter or encounters. And we return to the fact that there can be no love, no attraction without that first encounter. No one can love or be loved in a vacuum. And as I said before, your true love may be just around the corner.

My daughter married a young man she met in college. I met Milt at a summer resort in the Catskills where my mother and father had taken me and my sister since we were little girls. One of the producers with whom I work at NBC met his wife at NBC. Several of Milt's colleagues at Mt. Sinai Hospital married nurses they met at Mt. Sinai. Our insurance agent married the girl next door—a girl he had teased and tormented all through school. An editor I know met her first husband at the publishing house where they both worked. Her second husband was introduced to her by old friends. And so it goes.

The very best way to meet a man or a woman with whom you can develop an intimate relationship is probably through friends. One study involving 1,000 married couples showed that most of them met through a mutual friend. But you cannot just sit back and wait for someone to introduce you to Prince or Princess Charming. If you don't take the first step, and probably the first dozen steps, nothing will ever happen.

When recently widowed or divorced women ask me

how to meet men, I give them two suggestions. The first is to buy stock (and you should probably plan to buy at least ten shares if you want a broker to cooperate with you) in a number of major corporations. And then attend their annual meetings. The majority of stockholders at these meetings are male, and they tend to be intelligent, concerned, and financially stable. It is easy to start conversations with your fellow stockholders. You all have something in common.

The woman who cannot afford this route to expanding her circle of acquaintances might be able to earn the money by following my other suggestion, which is to sign up with one of the employment agencies that supply temporary office help. This gives you a chance to meet dozens of people in a very short time—and get paid, too. The more people you meet, the greater the probability that you will meet someone interesting.

Another way to take the initiative is to entertain. Sunday-night suppers, Sunday brunches, cocktails, small dinner parties are all good ways to expand your social circle. Six to eight people are ideal for parties where you serve food. Any more and you will find yourself too busy with the cooking to be able to enjoy your guests. But with six to eight, you can have at least one couple with whom you feel very close and comfortable and one or two other couples—married or unmarried—whom you would like to know better. If you don't know a single man, there is no reason why you can't ask another woman. The days of balancing the sexes are long gone by.

Men tend to take even less initiative than women do. They are so geared to the dating life that when they don't know someone to date they sit at home in front of the TV and feel sorry for themselves. The man who seriously wants to meet a woman whom he can love and who might love him should polish his talents as a host. People will not expect too much of him. Dinner can be as simple as food sent in from the nearest fast-food emporium.

By entertaining, you establish social credit. Your guests have incurred an obligation. If they had a good time, they will return the invitation. (If they didn't— well, figure out what went wrong and guard against it next time.) One dinner party for five or seven other people should result in at least one or two invitations. And the more people you meet, the more opportunities you have to entertain—and the richer your life will become.

Once you put your mind to it, you will undoubtedly be able to think of at least ten ways that you can meet new people—men and women. Don't neglect making new friends of your own sex. They have brothers and sisters and married friends who know single men and women.

My advice—once again—is to make a list. Write down those ten ways you have thought of to meet new people and then go ahead and do it. Don't give up just because you went to the opening of the local little-theater group, or whatever, and did not meet anyone interesting. Keep on trying until you've gone right down your list. And if none of those ten ways worked, then make another list. The same rules that apply to success in business apply to success in meeting people.

Some people take a what's-the-use? attitude. They lack self-confidence.

Douglas had managed to convince himself he was unlovable. He was in his forties and divorced. His wife had remarried, but Douglas was living alone and hating it. He had dated after the divorce, but had not been able to establish any lasting relationship. He felt it was his own fault. He had failed in his marriage. He was losing his hair. He was dull. He had reconciled himself to the fact that he was not going to go much further in his company. Younger men were being promoted over his head. He enjoyed what he was doing and he was skilled at it, but the idea that he had come to the end of his potential depressed him. He could not think of any positive quality that he possessed.

"Why should anyone love me?" he asked. "I'm a has-been. I'm a never-was. And I'm dull." He was not dull. Well educated and well read, he loved music and used to play with an amateur string quartet which had broken up when the cellist was transferred to another city.

"Let me tell you a story," I said. "A true story about bleeding ulcers."

"That's my style," he said unhappily. "I talk about love and you immediately think of a story about bleeding ulcers."

"This is about love," I assured him, and I told him about an experiment with seventeen patients who were suffering from bleeding ulcers. The doctor divided them into two groups and gave each member of one group a sugar pill. He told each of them that he or she would feel much better in about two hours, since this was a very effective new drug.

He asked his nurse to give each member of the second group the same sugar pill, instructing her to tell them that it was an experimental medication that might help them feel better, but the tests were not complete.

The next day, six of the eight patients to whom the doctor had given the pill reported that they did indeed feel better. But out of the nine patients who had been given the pill by the nurse, only two said that it had helped them.

"Very interesting," said Douglas when I paused, "but what has that got to do with me?"

"It's got to do with authority," I said. "The patients who were given the pill by the doctor, a higher-authority figure who told them it was effective, believed they would feel better. Those given the pill by the nurse, a lower-authority figure who gave them no assurance that it would work, were not helped.

"This applies to love, Doug," I said. "What you believe is important. You are your own authority figure. If you believe that you are lovable, you will be loved. If you believe that you are unlovable, it will be extremely difficult for you to find love. You *are* a lovable person. There is no reason for you not to love and be loved. You must believe this.

"Many women would be happy to meet someone with your knowledge of music, your gentleness, your sense of humor—and your good job. You are a good catch, as the saying goes."

Doug went away grinning sheepishly, a little flattered, a little uncomfortable. But something started bubbling inside him. He took the first step. He went to work to reorganize the string quartet.

Some time later he told me, "I don't know if it was the story of the bleeding ulcers or more music in my life or just coincidence, but I do feel better about myself these days. And I'm starting to date again. Maybe I am lovable." He smiled as he said this last bit, but he meant it. And he is lovable. Now that he believes he is. And he is taking steps to find love now.

Getting out in the world and meeting people is only the beginning. The next step is to attract the people you meet. Don't leave it up to fate. Stack the deck in your own favor. I suggest you turn back to Chapter Seven and review the use of the halo effect with an eye to using it to attract members of the opposite sex. And then reread Chapters Sixteen, "How to Make People Do What You Want," and Seventeen, "The Manipulative Handbook." Being able to attract another person is a form of power, a very important form. And the same rules apply.

The most effective way to attract a member of the opposite sex is to represent a reward to that person. If you used the four-list technique given in the previous chapter to diagnose your love needs, you learned that the qualities and characteristics that the person you love and the person you used to love possess and that you do not possess were the key to their attraction for you. This made it a rewarding relationship. They filled a need, made you feel more complete. There are many, many ways of providing rewards.

Annette is beautiful. Calvin is proud to be seen with such an attractive woman. He thinks it increases his stature in the eyes of others. Annette is also amusing. She makes Calvin laugh. He always has a good time with her. It is a rewarding relationship for him. He is extremely attracted to her.

Eric makes Claudia feel feminine and desirable. He has a special smile for her. He is punctilious about small attentions. No matter how liberated she protests she is, he still opens the car door for her—and she loves it. When he comes to dinner, he brings flowers. Claudia has never known anyone before who made her feel so cherished. She finds Eric's company rewarding.

Then there is the coincidental reward. This is when a man and a woman always meet in the circumstances that are enjoyable. Their pleasure has as much to do with the circumstances as with each other. But since they associate each other with good times and pleasure, they find each other rewarding.

Jane and Ralph met for the first time in Vermont at an after-ski drinking party, where they discovered they had a number of mutual friends at the resort. It was a marvelous evening. A log fire roaring in the huge fireplace. Good company. Dancing to phonograph records. Lots of laughter.

The two of them and their friends went skiing at the same resort almost every weekend that winter. They skied together, danced together, spent hours talking in front of the fire. It could not have been more satisfying. Ralph and Jane found each other's company tremendously rewarding, although in truth it was the atmosphere and the setting that had given them the most pleasure at the beginning.

Another effective way to use rewards is to employ what psychologists call selective reticence and what laymen call playing hard to get.

Carl meets Arlene at a cocktail party. He thinks she is great and wants to get to know her, but there are other men hovering around her. He decides that selective reticence is his best bet for catching her attention. After a few pleasant words, he excuses himself from the group around Arlene and chats with someone else. However, before the party is over, he gets Arlene's telephone number from his hostess.

A couple of weeks later, he calls Arlene and asks her to the opening of a new exhibition at the museum. They have a good afternoon at the exhibition and both run into people they know. Carl suggests that they ask them to have dinner with them. This keeps the dinner conversation from being as personal as it might have been if Arlene and Carl had been alone.

During the whole afternoon and evening he has been a bit formal, very courteous. But the next time he asks her out he shows more personal interest in her, more warmth. He lets Arlene know that he likes her, thinks she is attractive, enjoys talking with her.

Arlene was only mildly interested in Carl when she met him, but now she is definitely attracted. His slow approach and the way he kept his distance caught her interest and made her think about him. It acted as a challenge. She wondered if he really was attracted to her or just thought she was mildly amusing as a companion, the kind of person one might ask to go to the museum on a Saturday afternoon.

If he had been too reticent, if he had not shown that he had been interested enough in her to get her telephone number, nothing would ever have happened. And if on their next date he had not shown a little more warmth and a desire to know her better, then the whole thing would probably have fizzled. But he was selective about how he displayed his interest in her—and it worked. His reticence intrigued her. And since most people link elusiveness with value, the elusive man or woman seems more worth the pursuit than one who is pursuing you.

Emily used a variation of this technique with Arnold. Arnold met Emily and thought she was wonderful. Emily thought Arnold was pretty nice too, but she played hard to get. When Arnold called, she was busy—most of the time. Arnold was not daunted. He kept asking her to dinner, to the movies, to drive to the country to look for a Christmas tree, to go discotheque dancing. And when she did accept, he was pleased out of all proportion. When Emily finally responded to his ardor, Arnold could hardly believe in his luck. He is convinced he has the most wonderful woman in the world. He almost has to believe this, because he invested such a tremendous amount of time and effort pursuing her. It is psychologically inevitable that he now justify his efforts by believing that Emily is someone extraordinary.

Ruby also played the elusive game, but with a twist. When she agreed to go out with Ricky, it was always in such a way that his expectations were frustrated.

When Ricky asked her to go out to dinner on Friday, she refused, but suggested that he come over to her house on Saturday for supper. "Just a pickup meal," she told him. Ricky was delighted. But when he arrived at Ruby's there were other guests. Her "pickup" meal was a buffet for twelve. Ruby was warm and welcoming toward him, but there was no opportunity to be alone with her.

When he asked her to the movies a few nights later, she accepted. After the film, Ruby said, "I hope you don't mind, but I promised my aunt I'd look in on her on the way home. She's just back from the hospital and she might need something." What could Ricky say? Ruby sat and chatted with her aunt for an hour, then exclaimed over how late it was. "I won't ask you in," she said to Ricky as he escorted her home. "It's late and we both have to get up and go to work in the morning."

Each time Ricky was frustrated, his original sexual interest was increased by the frustration. When Ruby finally showed that she was attracted to him it was doubly gratifying, because it reduced both frustrations. If she had shown her deep interest earlier, Ricky would not have been so exultant. During this period of frustration, he had learned to think of Ruby as not just desirable, but highly desirable.

Carl, Emily, and Ruby represented a greater reward to Arlene, Arnold, and Ricky than they would have if they had responded earlier. This technique will not work, however, if there is no original spark of interest. There is nothing to be gained by selective reticence if the other person considers you a hopeless clod from the word go. And it will never work if both parties are using it.

What is so new about playing hard to get? Is it not "better" and "fairer" to be more open in your feelings? Selective reticence, admittedly, is a manipulative technique. But the awareness of what one is doing and its psychological impact may help some men and women handle the early stages of a budding relationship more skillfully, particularly those men and women who are seeking love and have been unsuccessful up to this point. Most of these individuals are unskilled in human relations. And for them—for most people, in fact—a slower approach is usually wiser than plunging into an intimate relationship on short acquaintance. It gives both individuals concerned time to think about their feelings for the other. It is easier to break off a relationship in these early stages without emotional hurt and a loss of self-esteem that might inhibit a man or woman from pursuing another relationship. If all seems to go well, then both will value the relationship even more than they would have earlier. The pursuer because he/she has his/her reward; the pursued because she/he has her/his reward—the warm knowledge of being deeply desired. And in these cases, attraction is indeed the first stage of love.

No matter how wary a man or woman may be about displaying interest in someone of the opposite sex too early, too openly, or too strongly, there are signs that are dead giveaways of attraction. One may not be aware of them on a conscious level, but the subconscious senses them. This is what keeps the Carls, Arnolds, and Rickys in hot pursuit.

One example: he or she will keep moving closer and closer to you until he/she is standing or sitting beside you. Then there is a physical reaction that one researcher describes as "a small backward leap of the torso." If someone gives that small backward leap while talking to you and looking into your eyes, you may be sure that he or she is attracted to you.

Eyes are love's tattletales. Dr. Zick Rubin, a psychologist who has studied many aspects of love and attraction, discovered that people who are attracted to each other spend much more time gazing into each other's eyes than men and women who are not. If you want to help things along, arrange to see the person who appeals to you in dimly lighted rooms as often as possible. Choose restaurants with subdued lighting. Serve dinner by candlelight. Have your after-dinner drinks by firelight—or moonlight. Replace those 100-watt bulbs with 25-watt rose-colored bulbs when he or she is coming over. In dim light the pupils of your eyes become larger, and that gives you a more seductive or loving look.

There are other ways to encourage the deepening of attraction. You can make the calendar your ally. Scientists have discovered that women tend to fall in love halfway through their menstrual cycle. Their sex drive is at its peak at this time. In these days when women are so frank about their periods, it is not difficult for a man to discreetly find out the date of a woman's last period and make his dating plans accordingly. And you can consult the moon as well. It is no mistake that the moon has been linked with romance over the centuries. Both men and women are more likely to fall in love at the times of the full moon and the new moon than at any other times.

So, gentlemen, if you ask a woman out halfway through her menstrual cycle on the night of the full moon and take her to a dimly lit restaurant, well, who knows? It might be the beginning of a great romantic love.

And there is something else, something intangible. If a man is attracted to a woman, if a woman is attracted to a man, there is a secret electricity between them. It may be weak at the start, but it is there. And each of them knows it. Oh, there may be exceptions—the very shy person who adores from afar, the immature soul who has a hopeless crush—but the average person with a healthy interest in the opposite sex and a desire for love will know when he or she has made contact.

This first stage of love, with its sexual excitement, the heady pleasure of being desired by another, is a very special "getting to know you" time. The couple tend to go from euphoria to despair and back again—usually not at the same time. And then there comes a period when the emotional depths are no longer so deep and the peaks are no longer so high. This is when infatuation and attraction grow into love or subside into indifference.

And if it is love, when the warmth and the concern and the excitement deepen, when the caring becomes more tender and unselfish, it is wonderful. For love is the ultimate goal. To love is the ultimate gift. And to be loved the ultimate reward.

CHAPTER TWENTY-FOUR

The Ultimate Goal

When you have found the man or woman whom you recognize as your true love, the person you want as a companion for the rest of your life, who will inspire you to do your best, who will give more meaning to your life, provide a center for your world; a person you find sexually and intellectually exciting, who can laugh with you, rejoice with you, hearten you, and cry with you at those times when tears must flow; a person who loves you and wants to work with you to build a relationship in which you both will find security, love, and the strength to fulfill yourselves, you are indeed blessed.

Love is the most powerful psychological tool. And a wonderful one. It brings out the best in us. And it may be the ultimate form of power. Love is manipulation in reverse—when we think not of what we want, but of what the other person wants and how we can help him or her gratify that want. There is a certain grandeur in this that does not exist in the mightiest concentration of political, financial, or other worldly power. This is the power of human fulfillment.

Love comes when manipulation stops; when you think more about the other person than about his or her reactions to you. When you dare to reveal yourself fully. When you dare to be vulnerable.

And that is the great secret of love. To allow oneself to be vulnerable. It is also the most courageous leap into the unknown that the spirit can make. But to gain and keep love, you must dare to expose your inner self to the person you love. It takes courage to entrust yourself to another. And many people are afraid to do this. In a discussion of the trend toward cohabitation instead of marriage (in just five years, according to the Census Bureau, the number of unmarried men and women living together has doubled—gone from 654,000 to 1.3 million), psychologists, sociologists, and theologians saw the phenomenon as a manifestation of fear of loving.

As a psychologist, a woman, a wife, a mother, I feel passionately that one must have the courage to commit oneself totally. You cannot demand or command love, any more than you can demand or command happiness. It comes from giving, from opening yourself to another, from caring, from daring to be vulnerable. And the rewards are immeasurable. Your love grows minute by minute, becomes deeper and more fulfilling until it is truly a part of you, a source of courage and comfort, the one emotion that permeates the humdrum fabric of everyday life to make it meaningful and gilds the peak experiences.

And as love grows stronger, you discover that you

no longer are vulnerable, because your love has become your armor—protecting you, nurturing you, encouraging you, fulfilling you. The ultimate goal. And it can be yours.

Epilogue

"To laugh often and much, to win the respect of intelligent people and the affection of children; to earn the appreciation of honest critics and endure the betrayal of false friends; to appreciate beauty, to find the best in others; to leave the world a bit better, whether by a healthy child, a garden patch or a redeemed social condition; to know even one life has breathed easier because you lived. This is to have succeeded."

—RALPH WALDO EMERSON

The Success Potential Test

The Place: Any large uncluttered space. Your living room with the furniture pushed against the walls, your backyard, the hall of your apartment house, the school playground, etc.

The Participants: At least six people. No more than ten.

The Equipment: A child's ring-toss game or the equivalent.

The Procedure: Participants are told that the purpose of the test is to get the ring over the pin. Each one has five tosses. There are no other rules. A participant may stand as close to or as far away from the pin as he chooses.

How to Rate Success Potential: The player who stands so close to the pin that he can ring it easily has little or no motivation for success. Nor does the player who stands so far away he can't ring the pin more than once. But the player who stands somewhere between these two extremes—close enough so that he has a chance of ringing the pin and far enough away to make it challenging—is the man or woman with the greatest potential for success.

What if a Participant Has No Success Potential? There is no Pass or Fail for this test, no right or wrong. It is a diagnostic device, designed to spot a personality characteristic. Individuals who rate low on success motivation usually are noncompetitive and place a high value on creating a life rich in human relationships. And this is another kind of success.

Turn to Chapter Ten for an explanation of this test and for ways to increase your success potential.

ABOUT THE AUTHOR

Dr. Joyce Brothers, a noted psychologist, is an NBC Radio Network personality, columnist, author, business consultant, wife, and mother. She broadcasts on NBC Radio Network Monday through Friday. She is a regular columnist for *Good Housekeeping* magazine and writes a daily column for King Features Syndicate which is published in newspapers throughout the United States and internationally as well. Her books have been translated into twenty-six languages. She is a frequent guest on network television programs and is a daily news commentator for Cable News Network and NIWS, a syndicated television news service. A United Press International poll named her one of the ten most influential American women, and a survey conducted by George Gallup called her one of the "Ten Most Admired Women." Dr. Brothers is a graduate of Cornell University. She is married to Dr. Milton Brothers, an internist. They have a daughter, Lisa, and reside in New York.